Alex Ritsema

A DUTCH CASTAWAY ON ASCENSION ISLAND IN 1725

In memory of the Dutch historian Michiel Koolbergen (1953-2002) who found the truth after more than 270 years

Copyright 2006 by Alex Ritsema

All rights reserved.

No part of this book may be reproduced in any form or by any electronic or mechanical means, including information storage and retrieval systems, without written permission from the publisher, except by a reviewer who may quote passages in a review.

Published by Alex Ritsema, Deventer, The Netherlands

Some illustrations in this book were drawn with permission from Menken Kasander & Wigman Uitgevers, Leiden, The Netherlands, from the book by Michiel Koolbergen, *Een Hollandse Robinson Crusoë*. The other illustrations were made by the artist Anneke de Vries, http://www.annekedevries.nl/ .

The front- and back covers (including text) were designed by Alex Ritsema, using the standard services at www.lulu.com. The line drawing on the front cover was made by Anneke de Vries. The illustration on the back cover was made by G.D. Hoogendoorn and was drawn from the book *Zeemansleven* with permission form publisher Callenbach-Kampen - no further duplication allowed.

ISBN: 978-1-4116-9832-1

CONTENTS

PREFACE AND ACKNOWLEDGEMENTS _____ 5

CHAPTER 1. A Dutch castaway on Ascension in 1725: myth or reality? ___ 8

CHAPTER 2. Ascension Island around 1725, a hell on earth _____ 11

CHAPTER 3. How Michiel Koolbergen identified the Dutch castaway ___ 20

CHAPTER 4. c.1695-1725: Life of Leendert Hasenbosch, prior to his exile on Ascension _____ 27

CHAPTER 5. May to October 1725: Leendert Hasenbosch on Ascension, "set ashore as a villain" _____ 42

CHAPTER 6. May to October 1725: a summary of the castaway's stay on Ascension _____ 76

CHAPTER 7. January 1726: British mariners discover the diary on Ascension 83

CHAPTER 8. When, where and how did Leendert Hasenbosch die? _____ 87

CHAPTER 9. 1726-1728: Did Daniel Defoe fictionalise the Dutch diary? __ 92

CHAPTER 10. 1730 and 1978: the story of the Dutch castaway is faked __ 103

CHAPTER 11. The Dutch East India Company (VOC): a short history___ 110

CHAPTER 12. The VOC and the "detestable crime of sodomy" _____ 121

CHAPTER 13. The marooning of Leendert Hasenbosch, compared with other maroonings around 1700 _____ 127

EPILOGUE. Another Dutchman on Ascension _____ 136

LITERATURE_____ 142

PREFACE AND ACKNOWLEDGEMENTS

In March 2005 I chanced upon a book in the public library of my hometown Deventer, *Een Hollandse Robinson Crusoë. Dagboek van de verbannen VOC-dienaar Leendert Hasenbosch op het onbewoonde eiland Ascension A.D. 1725*. Translated into English, the title reads "A Dutch Robinson Crusoe. The diary of Leendert Hasenbosch, employee of the VOC (Dutch East India Company) who was banished on the desert island of Ascension, AD 1725". The book drew my attention immediately, for I happen to be a collector of information about small islands everywhere in the world, as to their history, geology, wildlife and so on. I started reading the book and I soon found out that it was brimming over with fantastic new information about Ascension, a remote island in the South Atlantic Ocean, on which I had spent ten days of holiday in August 2000. The story - or legend - of the Dutch castaway on Ascension in 1725 was not new to me, because I had read about it in *Ascension, the story of a South Atlantic island* (1972), by the British author Duff Hart-Davis. However, the Dutch book disclosed the full truth for the first time.

The author of the Dutch book was Michiel Koolbergen, a person so far unknown to me. One of the last pages of the book contained a sad note written by the author's brother Jeroen Koolbergen, telling that the author had died on 1 June 2002, less than a month after lung cancer had been diagnosed. The book was published posthumously in the autumn of that year. Jeroen Koolbergen had completed the work, in cooperation with the publisher, Paul Menken. After some searching in the Internet I found out that Michiel Koolbergen was only 48 years old when he died.

I sent a review of Koolbergen's book to the Ascension Island newspaper (*The Islander*) and so I made contact with Raxa Sukhtankar. Raxa soon convinced me it would be better to write a book myself.

In June 2005 I started writing this book, with the encouragement of Jeroen Koolbergen and Paul Menken. Frankly, I do not add all that much to Michiel Koolbergen's excellent book:

- of this book, chapters 3, 4, 7, 9 and 10 are for about 90 percent my rewritings or summaries of parts of Koolbergen's book (of 296 pages). Naturally, I checked many of Koolbergen's sources. As I expected, he turned out to have used his sources skilfully;
- I have written the other chapters independently, mainly depending on other sources than Koolbergen's book, although much information of those chapters can be found in Koolbergen's book as well;
- In chapters 2, 5 and 6 I give more background information about the biology of Ascension than Koolbergen did;
- In chapters 11 and 12 I give more background information about Dutch history than Koolbergen did.

On a few points, I do not fully agree with Koolbergen's analysis and I will inform the reader about those points. Jeroen Koolbergen assured me, that, if his brother Michiel would still be alive, he would have liked critical comments on his book, as well as the publication of his research in English.

I am grateful to a huge number of persons, all of whom helped and encouraged me.

Jeroen Koolbergen lent me some relevant books of his late brother. Paul Menken, the publisher of Michiel Koolbergen, allowed me to use all illustrations of Koolbergen's book.

Four British biologists have helped me with the biology of Ascension: Annette Broderick, Brendan Godley, Philip Ashmole and Myrtle Ashmole. A fifth biologist, Stedson Stroud from Saint Helena and living on Ascension, not only helped me with the biology of Ascension but he also helped me improving parts of chapter 5 of this book. One time, I had a one-hour telephone call with him, with a large map of Ascension in front of me!

Some proofreading of early versions of parts of my manuscript was done by Jeroen Koolbergen, Raxa Sukhtankar and Duff Hart-Davis (author of *Ascension, the story of a South Atlantic island* (1972)). However, for improvements in my style and grammar I owe the most to the American Edward E. Leslie (author of *Desperate Journeys, Abandoned Soles*, 1988) and to my friends Theo Kletter and Marion van Beek; Theo and Marion had done the same during the preparation of my first book, *Discover the Islands of Ireland* (1999).

Finally, I am very pleased to have Anneke de Vries as the illustrator of my book.

Deventer, The Netherlands, April 2006

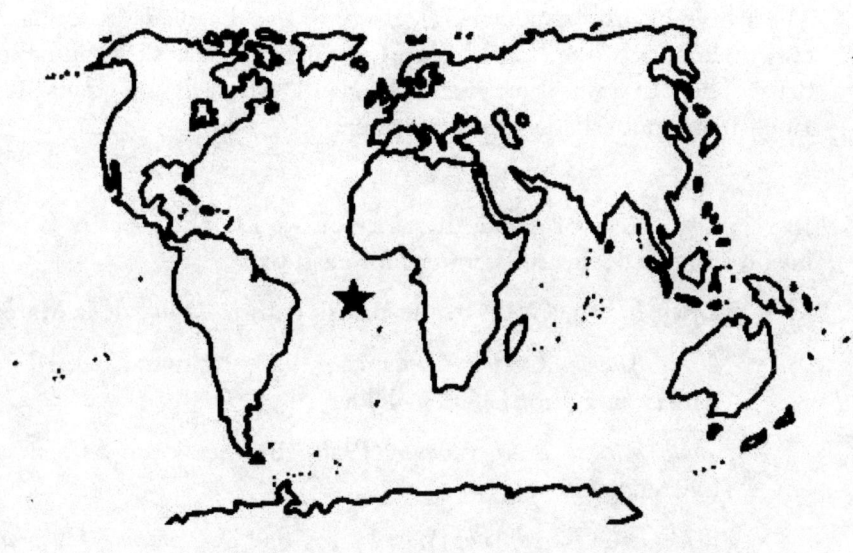

The star points to Ascension Island: not to scale, of course (from Koolbergen's book).

CHAPTER 1. A Dutch castaway on Ascension in 1725: myth or reality?

For more than two centuries there has been a story – or legend - of a Dutchman being utterly alone on Ascension Island[1]. On 5 May 1725 a Dutchman – on board a Dutch ship - was exiled to the uninhabited island, as a punishment for sodomy[2], a terrible crime in the United Provinces[3] in those days. The Dutchman was left behind with a survival kit that included a tent and a quantity of water. He wrote a diary, starting on 5 May 1725 and ending about half a year later. For food, the man had to kill turtles and seabirds, especially the easy-to-kill boobies. He soon ran out of his water supply and started desperate searches for fluids. The man must have had a guilty conscience, because he wrote about devils and demons that were confronting him with his former wrongdoings. The man's health quickly deteriorated and so he died. In January 1726 crew members of the English ship *Compton* found his skeleton next to his diary. The diary was brought to England, where it was translated into English and published some years later.

In varying degrees of detail, the story of the Dutch castaway is included in some books of the 20th century, for example:

- *Desert Islands* (1930), by the British author Walter de la Mare;
- *Great Shipwrecks and Castaways* (1952, reprinted 1991), by the American author Charles Neider;
- *South African Beach Comber* (1958), by the South-African author Lawrence Green;
- *Wideawake Island; The Story of the B.O.U. Centenary Expedition to Ascension* (1960), by the British author Bernard Stonehouse;

---

[1] For details about Ascension Island see chapter 2 and the epilogue.

[2] Sodomy was a contemporary collective term for all sexual activities not related to procreation. Usually, the contemporaries used "sodomy" for what we call "homosexuality" today. See chapter 13 for details.

[3] "United Provinces" was the contemporary expression for the country; the expression "The Netherlands" did not exist.

- *Islands Time Forgot* (1962), also by Lawrence Green;
- *Ascension, the story of a South Atlantic island* (1972), by the British author Duff Hart-Davis;
- *Desperate Journeys, Abandoned Souls* (1988, reprinted 1990), by the American author Edward E. Leslie.

In 1978 the American author Peter Agnos (pseudonym for Cy Adler) wrote a complete historic novel about the subject, *The Queer Dutchman* (reprinted in 1993). In this novel the castaway had got a name, captain, ship and so on. However, Agnos's book is a fake version of the castaway story, because Agnos *created* all 18th century Dutch documents and persons[4]. The late Michiel Koolbergen did not have much of a problem in proving *The Queer Dutchman* to be a fake but finding the name and background of the *real* castaway was something else. During the 1990s and the early 2000s Koolbergen patiently searched for the truth in Dutch and British archives and found the "Dutch Robinson Crusoe"! His name was *Leendert Hasenbosch*, an officer on board a Dutch ship and about 30 years of age when he was left behind on Ascension on 5 May 1725. Hasenbosch kept a diary that was found by British mariners in January 1726 and then brought to Britain. Koolbergen also found out that there were different 18th century English versions of the diary, none of which can be fully trusted. Of course, he would have liked to find the *original* Dutch diary but he did not succeed. If the original diary still exists, it is probably still in a dusty filing cabinet in Britain.

I will describe Koolbergen's detective work to identify the castaway as Leendert Hasenbosch in chapter 3. In later chapters I will describe the life of Leendert Hasenbosch and the publications of his diary. I will start with a description of the island of Ascension, as it was in the 18th century.

---

[4] For his book, Agnos even created a Dutch friend who would have done the translation work for him. See chapter 10 for details.

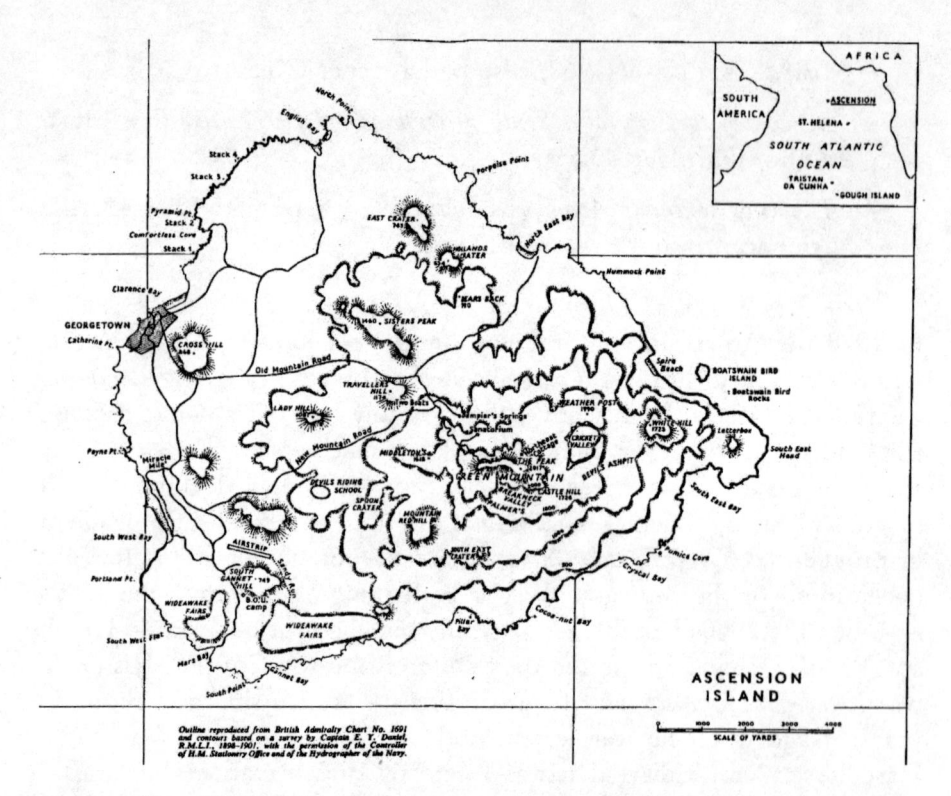

Ascension Island, on British Admiralty Chart No.1 (from Koolbergen's book). In the upper right corner we see the location of the islands of Ascension, Saint Helena and Tristan da Cunha between Africa and South America. The island's maximum length is about 10 kilometres. In the 18th century the usual anchoring spot was Clarence Bay, in the northwest, slightly north of modern Georgetown, the island's main village. This map shows roads and Georgetown; of course, roads and villages did not yet exist in the 18th century.

CHAPTER 2. Ascension Island around 1725, a hell on earth

Nowadays, Ascension Island is a British dependency and can be conveniently reached by passenger planes of the Royal Air Force or on a cruise with the Royal Mail Ship *Saint Helena*. Although Ascension is by no means a top tourist resort, the island has accommodations, shops and pubs to welcome visitors[5]. However, in the 18th century the island was quite inhospitable.

Ascension is a remote island, situated some 900 kilometres south of the equator, in the South Atlantic Ocean, about halfway between Africa and South America. The island has a maximum length of about 10 kilometres and a size of about 97 square kilometres (in comparison, Jersey, the largest of the Channel Islands, measures 116 square kilometres). As a result of little rainfall, Ascension is very dry and barren. Most of the island's eastern and southern shores consist of cliffs. The eastern part of the island is quite high and difficultly accessible. In the west we find a reasonably flat landscape with many volcanic cones with craters. On the western shores are some sandy beaches, interrupted by extensive lava fields or "clinker". Ascension's top rises to 859 metres and is called Green Mountain. Nowadays, the name "Green Mountain" is appropriate because of the numerous imported trees and other vegetation but in the 18th century vegetation was much scarcer.

Ascension was discovered by Portuguese mariners in 1501 and rediscovered by mariners from other countries in the following decades. Somewhere during the 16th century goats[6] were introduced, in order to

---

[5] For modern Ascension, as well as the personal visits to the island by Michiel Koolbergen and me, see the epilogue.

[6] In a Dutch book published in 1601 we read about *pigs* (!) on Ascension that would have been seen by mariners from the Dutch East India ships *Amsterdam* and *Utrecht*. On 30 and 31 May 1600. The – printed - text was written by an unknown writer on board the *Amsterdam*. The non-printed journal of the *Utrecht*, written by officer Reijer Cornelisz also wrote about the observation of two pigs. Cornelisz wrote there should be many more pigs on the island, according to the paths the pigs would have made (Koolbergen, *Ibid*, pp.120-125 and J. Keuning, *De Tweede Schipvaart naar*

provide fresh meat for future ship crews. Although the island was on the important sea route from the East Indies to Europe, it remained uninhabited until 1815. The main reason Ascension was ignored was, of course, its lack of fresh water. Other landmarks on route from the East Indies to Europe were considered far more important. For example, the Cape of Good Hope became a Dutch colony in 1652 and the island of Saint Helena became an English colony in 1659. Some contemporary sources suggest that Ascension was occasionally used as a place of exile for criminal mariners. However, the case of Leendert Hasenbosch – the main subject of this book - is the only documented case of such an exile[7].

In the 18th century, one of the prime reasons to stop at Ascension was to collect turtle meat. Many females of the green turtle (*Chelonia mydas*), a marine species of turtle, laid - and still lay - their eggs on the beaches of Ascension, where they were an easy prey for sailors. The turtles (weighing up to 250 kilograms[8]) were turned on their backs and brought on board alive. The contemporary expression was not "hunting" or "killing" turtles but "turning" them! The animals could be kept alive up to six weeks, until the cook slaughtered them.

Oost-Indië onder Jacob Cornelisz. van Neck en Wybrant Warwijck 1598-1600, part III, 1942, pp.XLVII-LIV).

[7] Duff Hart-Davis, in *Ascension, the story of a South Atlantic island*, p.13 wrote that a book of the Dutch traveller Jan Jansz Struys stated that the English were often using the island as an open prison for malefactors. By reading the text of Struys, published in Amsterdam in 1676, I conclude that Struys did *not* write so. The rest of Hart-Davis's summary of the text of Struys is correct: in 1673 the English made some 300 Dutch prisoners of war on Saint Helena and the English seriously thought of leaving them behind on Ascension. The Dutch would get some food and would be rescued by their own ships. However, when the English realised there was very little fresh water on the island, they decided to transport the Dutch prisoners to England where they set them free. As far as I know, there are only two other contemporary authors writing about Ascension as an open prison: the German author C.F.Behrens (see chapter 3 for details) and the Swedish author Per Osbeck (see chapter 8 for details).

[8] We should keep in mind that turtles generally continue to grow during their lifetime. The Ashmoles wrote in *St Helena and Ascension Island: a natural history* (p.198) that the female turtles on the beaches of Ascension weighed some 250 kilograms in the 18th century. The Ashmoles wrote to me that this was a very cautious estimate. The British author Ellis (1885) and the German author Krummel (1892) were writing about weights between 200 and 400 kilograms. In his Monograph *Ascension Island and Turtles* (1997), Roger Huxley wrote that a company butchering the animals measured an average of only 91 kilograms in 1931. This extremely low weight should be explained by the butchering in the previous decades. In 2002 researchers of the University of Exeter measured an average of 163 kilograms, with a range from 107 to 243 kilograms.

In the 18th century Ascension was a paradise for hundreds of thousands of breeding seabirds. Nowadays, their number is much lower, as a result of introduced rats, cats and dogs. Very easy to approach and kill were the large seabirds called boobies. The name "booby" was invented by English mariners and is quite appropriate![9] However, we do not read so much about systematic hunts of birds in the 18th century. Neither do we often read about goat hunting, perhaps because the goats were generally in the high regions in the interior of the island. The most important animals of Ascension – excluding marine mammals such as dolphins – are summarised in the table at the end of this chapter.

In the 18th century most ships calling at Ascension anchored in Clarence Bay in the northwest, in the area dominated by Cross Hill, a volcanic cone rising to 270 metres that often had - and still has - a large cross on its top. On the landside, Clarence Bay was - and is - enclosed by a long sandy beach, appropriately named Long Beach nowadays. Boats were needed to get ashore, which could be hazardous due to high waves and perilous undertows[10]. On the south side of Long Beach there was a rock formation, separating the beach from another sandy beach, called Deadman's Beach[11]. Hollows in the rock formation between the two beaches were sometimes used to leave messages behind. Nowadays, the rock formation between Long Beach and Deadman's Beach is no longer visible due to the fort and the pier that have been constructed at the same location. In fact, the entire landscape of this area has changed, because of the building of Georgetown, the island's main village.

In 1701 the English ship *Roebuck* was wrecked within view of Ascension. All men of the *Roebuck* managed to stay alive. The *Roebuck* was commanded by the renowned Englishman William Dampier (c.1652-1715), explorer and author. He was once a buccaneer but by 1701 he had become a gentleman.

---

[9] The Frenchman Robert Challe, bookkeeper on board a French East India Man, once wrote that beating one bird to death was almost an invitation to other birds to come closer! See Koolbergen, *Ibid*, p.139 and Challe, *Journal d'un voyage fait aux Indes orientales*, part 2, p.223

[10] For example, on 30 May 1600 the boat of the Dutch ship *Utrecht* capsized in Clarence Bay and the men almost drowned (Koolbergen, *Ibid*, p.123, same data as under footnote 5).

[11] J.E. Packer, in *A Concise Guide to Ascension Island* assumed that Deadman's Beach got its sinister name from the main cemetery in its neighborhood. In the 19th century there seems to have been a storm breaching the cemetery walls and washing bones and skulls out onto the beach.

On 21 February 1701, on her homeward voyage, the *Roebuck* came within sight of Ascension. The next day, the *Roebuck* got a serious leak and so the crew had to work desperately at the pumps for the rest of the day and night. In the morning of 23 February the ship anchored in Clarence Bay where she went down in about 48 hours. In fact, Dampier's descriptions in his book *A Voyage to New Holland* are so vague, that the exact location of the wreck remained unknown until divers from the West Australian Maritime Museum located it in March 2001. Before the *Roebuck* went down, Dampier and his men managed to salvage water, rice, chests, bedding, sails and so on. When Dampier and his officers, as the last ones, set foot on shore, they found part of the water and rice already stolen. On 26 February Dampier sent some men out to explore the island. The men soon found the island's most important water spring, in Breakneck Valley[12], to the southeast of the island's summit. The same spring would be crucial for the first colonists more than a century later. Ascension also has another source of fresh water, located on a lower spot in about the middle of the island, to the northwest of the island's summit. Interestingly, this spot is called "Dampier's Drip", because it was once believed to have been the water spring for Dampier and his men. Dampier's Drip – which is near a large cave called "Dampier's Cave"- is a much poorer source of water than the spring in Breakneck Valley.

How did Dampier's men find the water spring in Breakneck Valley? Dampier's book does not inform us but tradition has it that Dampier's men found the water spring by following a goat or perhaps a goat track[13].

---

[12] Hart-Davis, *Ascension, the story of a South Atlantic island*, p.15

[13] Hart-Davis, *Ibid*, p.16. The anecdote of the goat leading Dampier's men to the water spring – which might be true - was already mentioned in the diary of the London merchant Francis Rogers, written in 1703 and 1704, but published as late as 1936, in *Three Sea Journals of Stuart times [The diary of Dawrey Cooper; The journals of Jeremy Rock; The diary of Francis Rogers;* ed. B.S. Ingram], London, 1936; Koolbergen mentioned the story of Francis Rogers in *Ibid*, pp.275-276. There is also another anecdote related to Dampier's stay on Ascension, notably that he, being a privateer, would have buried a treasure on the island. This "anecdote" could better be called a "legend", because it cannot be true. Firstly, in spite of the romantic stories, privateers rarely buried treasures on remote islands or coasts. Secondly, in 1701 Dampier had already said farewell to his career as a privateer and had become a gentleman inside English upper circles. For example, among Dampier's friends or acquaintances were renowned men as the diarists Samuel Pepys and John Evelyn, the satirist Jonathan Swift and Daniel Defoe (Diana Souhami, *Selkirk's Island*, 2001, p.36).

Of course, Dampier's men also needed food and for that purpose they killed turtles, land crabs[14], seabirds and goats.

Dampier wrote that he and his men saw two ships about a week after the loss of the *Roebuck*. On 2 April 1701, they even saw eleven sails at the horizon, but none of them stopped[15]. One day later, after six weeks on the island, Dampier and his men were finally rescued by three British warships. The ships stayed at Ascension for some days – perhaps to turn turtles – and then sailed home, having spread the men of the *Roebuck* over the three ships.

In his book *A Voyage to New Holland*, Dampier was, unfortunately, very short and vague in describing his way of survival on Ascension. Perhaps Dampier wished to forget this episode of his life, because the loss of the *Roebuck* had cast a slur on his reputation. After homecoming, Dampier was court-martialled for both the loss of his ship and his decision to imprison his First Lieutenant, who - it appears - had some very influential relatives. Dampier was found guilty and was fined all his pay for the voyage; it was also declared that he should not command a King's Ship ever more. It is perhaps an indication of the respect held for Dampier that within a year he was anew in command of a King's Ship on a voyage of exploration[16].

We can be very sure about one thing: in the 18th century Ascension Island offered a single man little chance of survival.

---

[14] The land crab of Ascension, *Gearcinus lagostoma*.

[15] Michiel Koolbergen, *Ibid*, on page 275, wrote that Dampier and his men almost certainly saw the Dutch return fleet, under commodore Kornelis Koleman, consisting of eleven ships that had left Capetown on 16 March 1701, which was 5 March for the English, with their old "Julian" calendar. The travel time from Capetown to Ascension was in those days about a month, so it is almost certain that Dampier observed the Dutch fleet on 2 April 1701.

[16] See e.g. Graham Avis in http://www.heritage.org.ac/avis1.htm; Dampier, *A voyage to New Holland*, 1939 edition, pp. xlvi-l; Lloyd; *William Dampier*, London 1966, pp.93-96

Animals of Ascension around 1725		
Breeding seabirds	**Scientific name**	**Remarks**
Masked Booby	*Sula dactylatra*	
Brown Booby	*Sula leucogaster*	
Red-footed Booby	*Sula sula*	
Sooty Tern	*Sterna fuscata*	modern name on Ascension: Wideawake Tern
White Tern	*Gygis alba*	
Ascension Frigatebird	*Fregata aquila*	
Red-billed Tropicbird	*Phaeton aethereus*	modern name on Ascension: Red-billed Boatswain Bird
White-tailed Tropicbird	*Phaeton lepturus*	modern name on Ascension: Yellow-billed Boatswain Bird
Brown Noddy	*Anous stolidus*	
Black Noddy	*Anous minutus*	
Breeding marine reptile		
Green turtle	*Chelonia mydas*	

Animals of Ascension around 1725 (continued)		
Land mammals		
Black Rat	*Rattus rattus*	introduced[17]
House Mouse	*Mus musculus*	introduced[18]
Goat	*Capra hircus*	deliberately introduced in the 16th century
other land animals		
Land crab	*Gecarcinus lagostoma*	endemic species
Coconut-palm Gecko	*Hemidactylus mercatorius*	Perhaps introduced by Man, perhaps some individuals came on rafts

---

[17] Perhaps the Black Rat came as a result of the shipwreck of the *Roebuck* in 1701. Leendert Hasenbosch mentioned rats in his diary, in an entry of 19 August 1725; see Chapter 5.

[18] Philip and Myrtle Ashmole wrote to me that the House Mouse was certainly present by 1754, although that information was not in their standard work *St Helena and Ascension island: a natural history*. Perhaps this species came along with the rats, perhaps as a result of the shipwreck of the *Roebuck* in 1701.

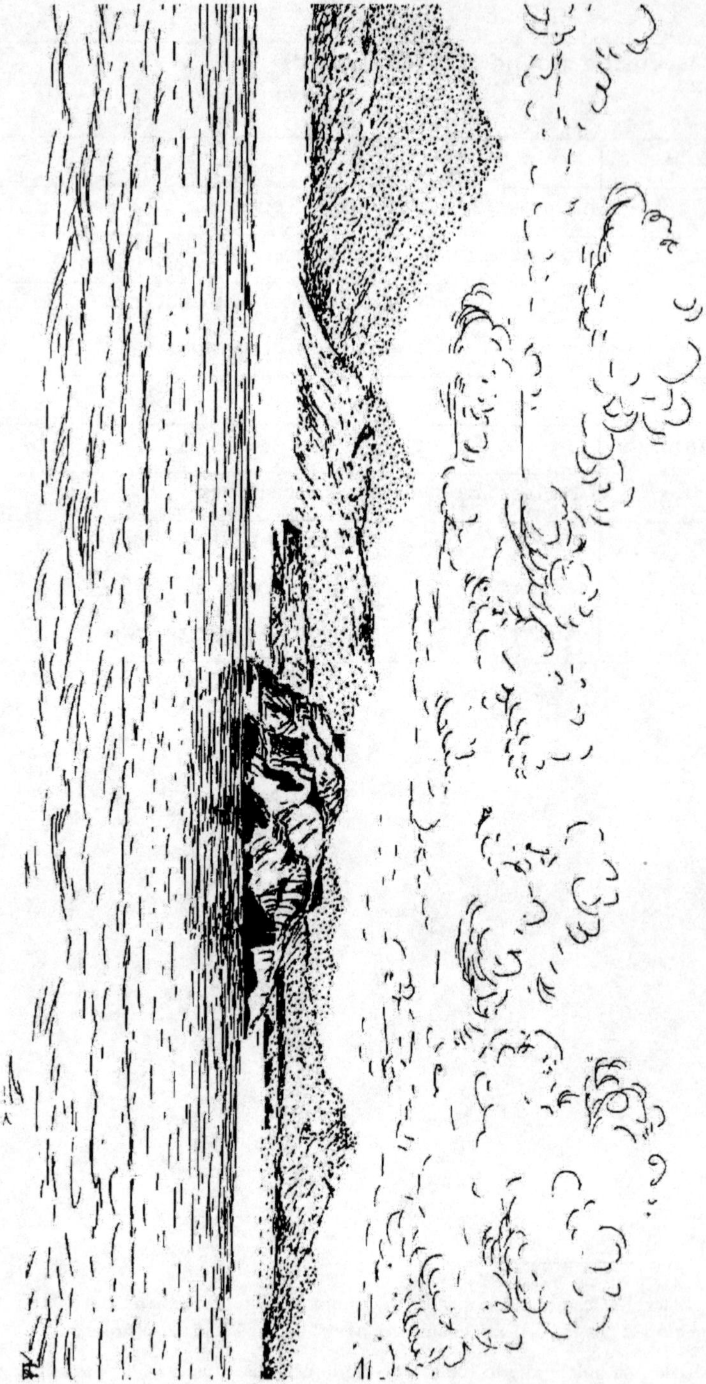

(Caption to picture on the previous page: the drawing by Anneke de Vries, from a drawing in Koolbergen's book, adjusted)

Here we see the landing spot of Ascension, as it might have looked like in 1725. To the left we see the high top of Cross Hill. In 1725 there was no cross on Cross Hill, although there had been one before. On a modern picture from this perspective we would see many buildings of Georgetown. Part of Long Beach is visible in the left (north); part of Deadman's Beach is visible in the right (south) of the picture. Caves in the rock formation between the two beaches were used as post boxes. The Dutch castaway seems to have slept in one of the caves during his first nights. The rock formation is no longer visible, because of a fort and the landing pier.

According to Duff Hart-Davis, in Ascension, the story of a South Atlantic island, *in 1693 some visitors saw something they had not expected, notably a cross on the hill that is now called Cross Hill. The cross was probably meant as a beacon, but was not always present.* In his diary as published in An Authentick Relation *(see chapters 5 and 6)* Leendert Hasenbosch did not mention a cross on the top of Cross Hill; if a cross had been there, he would, almost certainly, have written so in his diary. The log of the English East India Man Compton, *whose crew found the diary of Hasenbosch in January 1726, also explicitly mentioned "the Cross that was on the Hill is taken down" (see also chapter 7). From these data we may perhaps draw the cautious conclusion that the island was not often visited around that time.*

*A female Green Turtle (*Chelonia mydas*) in her nest on a sandy beach: only the females get on land (drawing by Anneke de Vries, from a photo by Annette Broderick).*

CHAPTER 3. How Michiel Koolbergen identified the Dutch castaway

Michiel Koolbergen liked mariner's tales. Once, he discovered an old booklet in the library of the Amsterdam Maritime Museum, entitled *An Authentick Relation*[19]. The booklet was published in English in 1728 but included a diary of a Dutch sailor, who had been banished to the desert island of Ascension a few years before the publication. Koolbergen's first reaction was: could this man have been a *real* Dutch Robinson Crusoe, a *real* man trying to survive on an island on his own? The complete title of the booklet that inspired Koolbergen was:

> *An Authentick Relation of the many Hardships and Sufferings of a Dutch Sailor, Who was put on Shore on the uninhabited Isle of Ascension, by Order of the Commadore of a Squadron of Dutch Ships. – with – A Remarkable Account of his Converse with Apparitions and Evil Spirits, during his Residence on the Island. - and – A particular Diary of his Transactions from the Fifth of May to the Fourteenth of October, on which Day he perished in a miserable Condition. – Taken from the Original Journal found in his Tent by some Sailors, who landed from on Board the Compton, Captain Morson Commander, in January 1725/6.*

The long title gives some interesting information, such as exact dates. Koolbergen decided to check the dates given in both the title and the main text. When reading the dates on the title page, one must assume that the Dutch sailor was marooned on Ascension in the year 1725. The first date in the main text of the diary was "Saturday, May 5" and Koolbergen soon discovered that 5 May 1725 was a Saturday indeed. To be precise, 5 May 1725 was a Saturday in the *modern* or *Gregorian* calendar that was already used in the United Provinces in 1725, while the British still used the *old* or *Julian* calendar that ran eleven days behind the modern calendar. Moreover, in Britain the New Year started on 25 March instead of 1 January, which explains the odd-looking notation "January 1725/6" in the last sentence of the long title.

---

[19] The complete text is in chapter 5 of this book.

The diary in *An Authentick Relation* does not reveal the author's name or the name of his captain or the name of the ship that had brought him to Ascension. In fact, the diary does not give any names of persons or ships at all. When reading the booklet, Koolbergen soon concluded – as many other people had done before him[20] - that the Dutchman was left behind on the desert island as a punishment for sodomy. In fact, the entire diary has a homosexual theme. For example, the narrator does not tell anything about a woman, let alone a wife or girl friend. The clearest reference to homosexuality can be found in an entry of 20 June 1725:

> my most heinous Crime of making use of my Fellow-Creature to satisfy my Lust, whom the Almighty Creator had ordain'd another Sex for.

Under the same date, the narrator also wrote about the apparition of the ghost of a deceased friend, with whom the author might have had a homosexual relationship:

> (…) when he was in this World we were as great as two own brothers. He was a Soldier at Batavia.

In fact, "Batavia" and "Ascension" are the *only* names that can be found in the entire diary.

If the diary were genuine, Koolbergen realised, it would mean that the castaway must have been on board a ship of the VOC, the Dutch East India Company, being the only Dutch company with ships approaching Ascension. Moreover, the castaway's ship must have been *homebound*, because the island was not on the outbound routes.

Koolbergen also drew an important conclusion from the very first sentence of *An Authentick Relation*, which reads:

---

[20] Although those other people generally used another version of the diary than the diary published as *An Authentick Relation*. Details about the unreliable rewritings of *An Authentick Relation* will be described in chapter 10. However, the homosexual theme appears in all versions.

> Saturday, May 5. By Order of the Commodore and Captains of the Dutch Fleet, I was set on Shore on the Island of Ascension, which gave me a great deal of Dissatisfaction, but I hope Almighty God will be my Protection.

After he had studied the legal practices of the VOC, Koolbergen concluded that the statement "Commodore and Captains of the Dutch Fleet" was in line with the legal practice in a convoy of VOC-ships. In such a convoy there was a *Breede Raad* (literally Broad Council), consisting of the commodore and the captains of all convoy ships, to deal with serious crimes, such as sodomy, mutiny or murder.

Of course, Koolbergen tried to find the logs of all homebound VOC-ships in the year 1725, hoping to find evidence that the *Breede Raad* had sentenced someone to exile on Ascension. At the VOC-archives in The Hague, Koolbergen easily found the names of all homebound VOC-ships of 1725, a convoy of twenty-three ships, commanded by commodore Ewout van Dishoeck. Unfortunately, *all* twenty-three logs of the homebound fleet turned out to be missing. The logs - as many other documents of the VOC - were probably sold as waste paper somewhere in the 19th century[21].

Without the logs of the ships, Koolbergen had to search for other sources of information. After having studied the VOC in general, Koolbergen found out that Commodore Ewout van Dishoeck, after coming home, had to attend two meetings in order to justify his deeds; one meeting with the *Heeren Zeventien* (literally "Lords Seventeen" or the High Commanders) of the VOC and another meeting with the *Staten-Generaal* (the Dutch Parliament). Koolbergen found the records of both meetings in the official archives. Unfortunately, none of the records contained any information showing that the *Breede Raad* had sentenced anyone to banishment on Ascension. But Koolbergen realised that the lack of documentary evidence did not mean that a marooning on the

---

[21] It is possible, that some of the logs are still in private archives in The Netherlands, with the present owner(s) not even knowing it.

island had not occurred. For example, it was possible that all references to a trial for sodomy had been kept out of the minutes[22].

Fortunately, Koolbergen found useful information in the minutes of the meeting of Ewout van Dishoeck with the Dutch Parliament: the homebound fleet of 1725 left Cape Town on 11 April, passed the island of Saint Helena on 27 April and reached the island of Ascension on 3 May. All these dates could perfectly match the beginning of the diary of the unknown Dutchman on Ascension on 5 May. However, the entire diary published in *An Authentick Relation* could still be pure fiction.

When both sets of minutes had not delivered the desired result, the *salary logs* inside the VOC-archives seemed to be Koolbergen's last hope for crucial information. If a VOC-employee had been banished to Ascension, then the last entry of his salary log should mention the confiscation of his outstanding salary at the moment of the sentence[23]. Finding the names of all VOC-employees on board the homebound fleet in 1725 could be done by checking the salary logs of the thousands of VOC-employees in the East Indies in 1724, because all of them might have been on board that homebound fleet. However, checking the salary logs of all those thousands of people would be tedious and time-consuming indeed. Moreover, the clerks of the VOC generally sorted the employees under the name of the *outbound* ship that had brought them to Asia, sometimes many years before their homebound journey. Of course, many - if not most - VOC-employees sailed home on board *another* ship than the ship that had brought them to Asia[24].

---

[22] Koolbergen was convinced that Van Dishoeck must have orally informed the High Commanders of a meeting of the *Breede Raad* in case such a meeting had taken place, because the conviction of one of his officers would have implications for the administration. After the meeting, the High Commanders were content with Van Dishoeck's decisions. Van Dishoeck was given a golden chain and medal with a value of about 900 Dutch guilders, a usual reward for the commodores of homebound fleets. The High Commanders also allowed all Chambers of the VOC to pay the salaries of the officers who had come home, because there had been no complaints about them.

[23] VOC-employees on board generally saved their salary and did not cash it until they arrived in some port. Sometimes, VOC-employees also saved part of their salary by not cashing it for other reasons.

[24] For example, let us suppose a married corporal of the VOC left the home country in 1714 on board ship X and subsequently stayed for many years in Asia. The registration of all his promotions, his salary-payments, his gifts from his salary to his wife in the home country, etc. often remained sorted in the salary-logs under "ship X" until the end of his career, although the

Koolbergen got a hint when he read a German book published in 1737, *Reise durch die Sued-Laender und um die Welt* ("voyages through the south lands and around the world"), written by one Carl Friedrich Behrens. According to this book, the island of Ascension was sometimes used to set criminals ashore, as would have happened to a Dutch bookkeeper, guilty of sodomy. If Behrens's remark about the Dutch bookkeeper was correct[25], the unknown author of *An Authentick Relation* might have been *bookkeeper* on board of one of the homebound ships of the VOC in 1725! As every VOC-ship had only one bookkeeper - one of the officers - on board, Koolbergen's number of possible persons was suddenly reduced to twenty-three, provided it would be possible to track down the names of those twenty-three bookkeepers. When Koolbergen decided to exclude the ships that had not started their homebound voyage in Batavia (a place mentioned in *An Authentick Relation*), the number was further reduced to eighteen. At Koolbergen's request, someone employed at the VOC archives in The Hague tracked down the names of the eighteen bookkeepers. Fortunately, the eighteen names happened to be in some preserved VOC-documents written in Batavia in 1724, shortly before the fleet departed.

---

person involved had nothing to do with that ship any more ("ship X" might even have vanished in the meantime). Of course, the VOC-clerks in Asia sent all relevant information about the salary of the involved employee to the United Provinces as well. Koolbergen had to hope that the man he was searching for was not a member of a specific category of employees of the VOC, notably those employees who had never been on board an outbound VOC-voyage, such as employees who had been born in Asia. For most of those employees there were no salary data available in the archives in the Netherlands. Fortunately, Koolbergen's man turned out not to belong to that specific category.

[25] Koolbergen wrote that Behrens's book could not be fully trusted, because it mixed facts and fantasy. However, by presuming Behrens's remark about the Dutch bookkeeper was true, Koolbergen finally found what he was searching for. It will probably remain a mystery forever, how Behrens knew the Dutch castaway had been a bookkeeper. The crucial text (in 18th century German) about Ascension Island in *Reise durch die Sued-Laender und um die Welt*, 1737, page 250: "Es werden auch zuweilen grosse Verbrecher und schaendliche Missethaeter, auf diese Insul ausgesetzet, dergleichen auch einem gebohrnen Hollaender, der seiner Profession nach ein Buchhalter auf den Schiffen war, um veruebter Sodomiten willen, wiederfahren". In the French version of the text [*Histoire de l'expédition de trois vaisseaux, envoyés par la Compagnie de Indes Occidentales des Provinces-Unies, aux lettres Australes en MDCCXXI*], page 250, the crucial passage reads: "On y relegue quelquefois des maltraiteurs, comme il est arrivé à un certain teneur de livre, né Hollandois: il y fut exposé pour crime de Sodomie".

Koolbergen's next step was to find the salary logs of the eighteen bookkeepers of the homebound fleet of 1725, all of whom could have started their career at the VOC in another (lower) function and perhaps many years prior to 1725. After some time, Koolbergen found the "Dutch Robinson Crusoe": *Leendert*[26] *Hasenbosch* from The Hague, sailing home on board the ship *Prattenburg* in 1725, working as the bookkeeper of that ship, although he was officially only a clerk, a sort of minor bookkeeper, with a salary of sixteen guilders a month, six guilders less than a bookkeeper. The salary log of Leendert Hasenbosch ends with a statement, written - in stately 18th century Dutch - by some VOC-clerk in late 1725, after the *Prattenburg* had come home:

> *1725 – 17 april op prattenburg tot heden dat gecondemneert is om op het Eyland Asschentioen dan wel elders voor schelm aan de wal gejaagt te werden met confiscatie syner te goed hebbende gagie.*

Translated into modern English:

> On 17 April 1725, on the *Prattenburg*, he was sentenced to be set ashore, being a villain, on the island of Ascension or elsewhere, with confiscation of his outstanding salary.

Obviously, Leendert Hasenbosch was sentenced to exile on Ascension on 17 April 1725, a date that perfectly matches with the dates of the movements of the fleet: on 10 April the fleet left Capetown, on 27 April the fleet passed Saint Helena and on 3 May the fleet reached Ascension. Two days later, Leendert Hasenbosch was left behind.

So we now know his name and his profession. But what type of man was Leendert Hasenbosch?

---

[26] "Leendert" is Dutch for "Leonard".

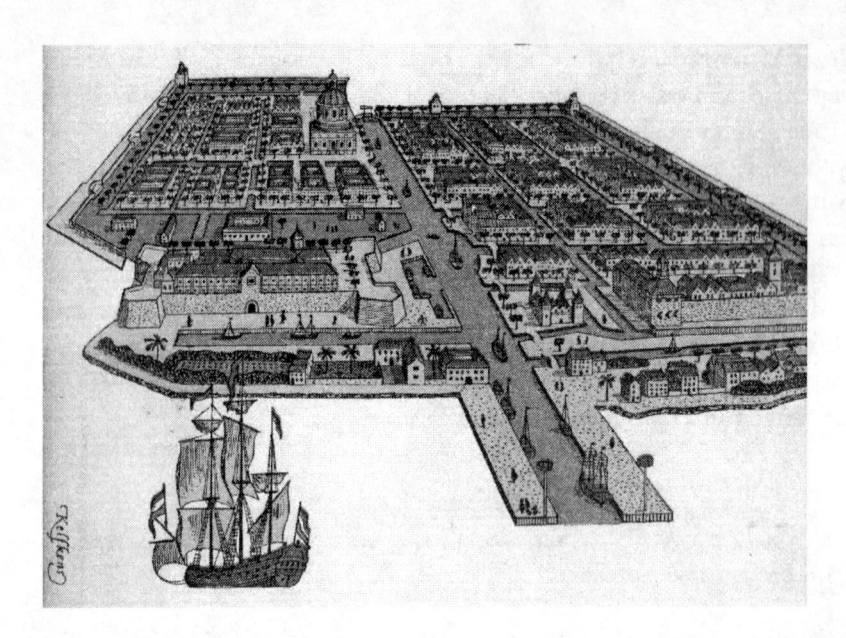

Batavia (now Jakarta) in the 18th century. Leendert Hasenbosch, the Dutch castaway of 1725 lived here as a VOC-employee, as a soldier between August 1714 and September 1715 and in higher ranks between August 1720 and November 1724 (from Koolbergen's book).

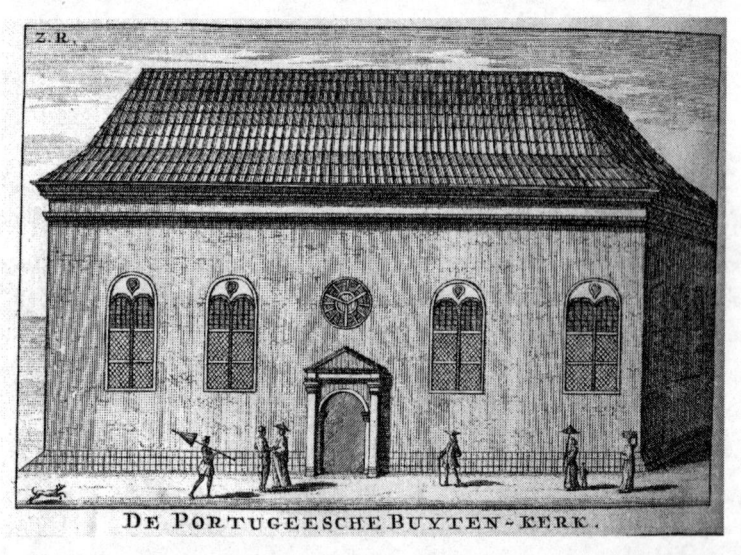

The Portuguese Outer Church in Batavia from a publication in 1727. We know for certain that Johannes Hasenbosch (1672-1723), the father of castaway Leendert Hasenbosch, was the sexton of this church at the time of his death; perhaps Johannes Hasenbosch had that function for many years (from Koolbergen's book).

CHAPTER 4. c.1695-1725: Life of Leendert Hasenbosch, prior to his exile on Ascension

Leendert Hasenbosch, the Dutch castaway on Ascension, was probably born in The Hague, probably in the year 1695. He was the only son of Johannes Hasenbosch (1672-1723) and Maria van Bergende (?-1707 (?)), who married in 1691. In the first years of this marriage, Johannes Hasenbosch seems to have made a living as a grocer. Perhaps he still was a grocer in later years but we have no reliable data. The children were probably all born in The Hague, in the following order:

- daughter Cornelia, born in 1692;
- daughter Ursula, probably born in 1693;
- daughter Helena, born and died in 1694;
- son Leendert, probably born in 1695;
- daughter Maria Elizabeth, probably born in 1696.

Shortly after the infant death of daughter Helena in 1694, the family seems to have switched from the Roman Catholic religion to the Dutch Reformed - Calvinistic – religion, which was a sort of State Church. Mother Maria died in 1706 or 1707.

In 1708 or 1709 father Johannes travelled to Batavia with his three daughters Cornelia, Ursula and Maria Elizabeth. Unfortunately, we do not know the precise date, the harbour of departure or the name of the VOC-ship that took them aboard as passengers. Neither do we know the father's motivation but presumably he wished to start a new life. When father Johannes and his daughters went to Batavia, son Leendert, aged about fourteen, stayed in the United Provinces. Perhaps father Johannes did not get permission to take his son with him, whereas his three daughters were quite welcome in Batavia, because of a perennial shortage of white female marriage partners in that town[27]. It seems likely that

---

[27] Koolbergen, *Ibid*, pp.67-87. All three daughters would marry and give birth to children in Batavia. Koolbergen managed to track down some dates of marriages, births and deaths of members of the Hasenbosch family, but a number of these dates remain unclear. The two eldest daughters stayed in Batavia: Ursula died somewhere between 1723 and 1726 and Cornelia died in 1735. Cornelia married no less than three times, which was not unusual in a town as unhealthy as

father Johannes sought some guardian or home for his son. Perhaps father Johannes also organised some education for his son. Unfortunately, we have no data at all.

The younger years of Leendert Hasenbosch and his family members might be a mystery forever. However, we are sure about one thing; at the end of 1713, Leendert Hasenbosch, aged about eighteen, became a VOC-soldier in Enkhuizen, with the normal - very low - salary of 9 guilders a month. We do not know why he started his career in Enkhuizen, a VOC-port further away from his birthplace The Hague than the VOC-ports of Delft, Rotterdam, Amsterdam and Hoorn. Perhaps he had already moved from The Hague. Upon his appointment, Hasenbosch received the usual two months salary in advance so that he could buy a soldier's uniform and standard equipment. The equipment consisted of a chest containing clothes, a tobacco box, pipes, a tinderbox, toiletries and cutlery. If the employee could read, the chest generally also contained a small bible or prayer book, as well as paper and writing materials[28]. Hasenbosch was lucky enough to leave the United Provinces without a debt to some dubious recruiter; many soldiers and sailors started their Asiatic adventure by accumulating a huge debt.

We can only speculate about the motivations of Hasenbosch to start a career as a soldier at the VOC, an organisation that had built up a reputation as a bad employer, especially for its lower personnel. The salaries were low, the working conditions were terrible and there was a substantial chance of dying young, on board a ship or in the unhealthy heat of the tropics. Most Dutch boys preferred starting a career ashore. Experienced Dutch sailors usually preferred sailing for other companies. As a result, about half of the VOC-soldiers and VOC-sailors were foreign-born[29].

Batavia. The youngest daughter, Maria Elizabeth, went back to the United Provinces as a widow; we do not know when, but she must have gone back before 1720.

[28] Koolbergen, *Ibid*, p.74.

[29] For more details about the VOC, see chapter 11.

Hasenbosch sailed to Batavia on board the VOC-ship *Korssloot*, which left the roadstead of the island of Texel[30] on 17 January 1714. Together with 27 other soldiers on board, Hasenbosch probably had little to do on board. Soldiers were a sort of passengers, whose service would start after arrival in the Eastern colonies. At sea, occasionally the soldiers had to assist the hard-working mariners. On board of VOC-ships quarrels and irritations between soldiers and mariners were very common but we know nothing about the atmosphere on the *Korssloot* whatsoever.

On 13 August 1714, after a successful voyage, the *Korssloot* reached Batavia. A few days later Hasenbosch and the other soldiers were transferred by boat to the *Waterpoort* (Water Gate) of the Castle of Batavia. After an official parade accompanied by music, the new soldiers were spread over the various guard posts, such as the Castle itself, the small fort nearby and the four town gates of Batavia.

Between August 1714 and September 1715 Hasenbosch was stationed in the Castle of Batavia itself. Almost certainly, his life was quite dull, with drillings, parades and being on patrol[31]. Not surprisingly, soldiers in Batavia were often drunk on the local alcoholic drinks. For example, there was a punch made of sugar, lemon and tamarind and a sort of beer made of sugar, lemon and arrack. Sometimes soldiers took over a service duty of a colleague for five *stuivers*, i.e. a quarter of a Dutch guilder. Soldiers were allowed to marry Asian women, provided those women had themselves baptised as members of the official Dutch (Calvinistic) religion. Married soldiers were allowed to spend the nights with their wives but single soldiers, such as Hasenbosch, had to sleep in the barracks and were allowed only one night off per week. A soldier who had been outside without permission could be severely punished. First, the soldier was heavily lashed and then he had to be on patrol for many hours, in the heat, with an iron helmet on his head! The punished soldier would have terrible headaches for many days to come.

---

[30] For anchoring purposes, the south shore of Texel Island was perfectly situated. VOC-ships of the ports of Amsterdam, Hoorn and Enkhuizen always had the problem of sailing over the shallow Zuyder Sea, on which the ships could not sail with full load. At the roadsted of Texel, the VOC-ships were loaded or unloaded with small inshore ships.

[31] About a soldier's life in Batavia, see Iong, *Het krijgswezen der VOC*, 1950, pp.80-88 and Els M. Jacobs, *De Vereenigde Oost-Indische Compagnie* , 1997, pp.182-183.

Cochin seen from the land (upper picture) and from the sea in the 18th century. Between 1715 and 1720, Leendert Hasenbosch was in or near Cochin, as a soldier of the VOC (Dutch East India Company) (from Koolbergen's book).

Hasenbosch was in Batavia when the town was blooming (1700-1730). The town had some 60,000 people, with a quite complex social structure. Only some 10 percent of the people in the city were white, although the whites - and especially the *Dutch* whites - were well represented in the upper classes. Life in the hot and humid town was not particularly healthy, not even for the upper classes.

Most whites were employees of the VOC and so white men grossly outnumbered white women. That is why many white men choose coloured wives. The largest population groups in the city were the Chinese and the slaves, deriving from all corners of Indonesia[32]. The town had several churches but for Protestants only. The preaching of other religions was strictly forbidden. For example, when Portuguese or Spanish ships called at Batavia, the Catholic priests on board of those ships were lodged in the Castle until the ships departed, because the Dutch authorities had bad experiences with secret Catholic masses, carried out in private homes!

Between August 1714 and September 1715 Hasenbosch might have visited his father or sisters, who were all living in Batavia at the time. For example, on 1 January 1715, a child of his youngest sister Maria Elizabeth was baptised in Batavia. According to the baptismal registers, Maria Elizabeth's father Johannes and her eldest sister Cornelia were witnesses at the ceremony. Perhaps father Johannes Hasenbosch made his living as the sexton of the so-called "Portuguese Outer Church", located southeast of the town, outside the city walls. We know for certain - from a preserved document - that Johannes Hasenbosch had that function at the time of his death, in July 1723. The Portuguese Outer Church was the church of a specific social group, the *Mardijkers*. A few generations before the stay of the Hasenbosch family in Batavia, the original *Mardijkers* had derived from various Asian groups and Portuguese half-breeds in some Portuguese colonies. The Dutch had brought those *Mardijkers* to Batavia as prisoners of war. After some time, they had become free people[33]. For generations, most *Mardijkers* kept speaking Portuguese and wearing clothes of Portuguese fashion.

---

[32] Els M.Jacobs, *Ibid*, p.189.

[33] The name *Mardijker* was derived from the Malay word *mardeka*, meaning "released person".

In September 1715 Hasenbosch was shipped to Fort Cochin on the Malabar Coast, the west coast of what would later be British India. In total, some 1500 VOC-soldiers were shipped to Cochin around that time. Not far from Cochin, an Asian samurin ("prince" or "king") had violated the interests of the VOC and so the VOC-authorities decided to organise a punitive expedition. Almost certainly, Hasenbosch was one of the VOC-soldiers involved in this punitive expedition, culminating in the bloody battle of Paponetty.

For the background of the battle of Paponetty, we have to go back to 1662 and 1663. In those years the samurin of Calicut had helped the VOC by expelling the Portuguese from Cochin and some less important forts along the coast, such as Cranganoor and Cannanoor. The samurin had probably hoped to become king of Cochin. However, the Dutch only granted him the less important fort Cranganoor, to the north of Cochin. In 1666 the Dutch even deprived him of this fort and so the relationship between the Dutch and the dynasty of samurins of Calicut quickly deteriorated[34]. In 1714 the Dutch even started building a fortress near Siltua on the long island of Chetway, which was only separated from the Calicut Empire by a river. Of course, the samurin regarded this Dutch action as a provocation but he decided not to act until the Dutch fort was almost complete. On 22 January 1715 the samurin sent 600 of his soldiers across the river to the island of Chetway, who easily took the Dutch fort, which was still under construction[35].

As an attempt to retake the island of Chetway, a Dutch punitive expedition was carried out by Barend Ketel, the commander of Malabar. This expedition failed and killed at least 80 VOC-soldiers. The samurin celebrated his victory by building a palisade with three enclosures, called Paponetty. Paponetty was soon occupied by East Indian military, as well as Portuguese mercenaries and English sergeants, who were very willing to subdue the power of the VOC.

---

[34] H.K. Jacob, in "De VOC en de Malabarkust in de 17de eeuw", in *De V.O.C.in Azië*, 1976, p.86.

[35] J.Canter Visscher, *Mallabaarse brieven, behelzende eene naukeurige beschrijving van de kust van Malabar*, 1743, pp.55-58.

After this humiliation, the VOC decided to prepare a much larger punitive expedition. And so, many soldiers, including Leendert Hasenbosch, were transported from Batavia to Cochin.

In January 1716 Barend Ketel led a new campaign against the samurin of Calicut, carried out with many new soldiers from Batavia. On 11 January the expedition approached the palisade of Paponetty. The Indian soldiers and their few Portuguese and English allies soon left the palisade on the other side. The Dutch could have claimed an easy victory. However, one Dutch captain, named Pluis, thought the retreat of the enemy to be a tactical manoeuvre meant to attack the Dutch from the rear, so the Dutch decided to withdraw. Afterwards the East Indians, Portuguese and English retook the palisade, again humiliating the Dutch. The Dutch were afraid of losing all their holdings in Malabar. For example, it was rumoured that some local princes, who had cooperated in the pepper trade for many years, wanted to attack the Dutch fort at Cranganoor.

In November 1716 a new group of VOC-soldiers -Europeans and East Indians - from Batavia, arrived in Cochin. The number of Dutch military in Cochin now exceeded 3,000 men. A new punitive expedition, with about 3,400 VOC-soldiers, was started under the command of Willem Bakker Jacobz. Bakker had previously sent letters to various local princes, announcing his arrival and his intention to punish the samurin of Calicut. Early in the morning of 16 January 1717 Bakker gave orders to attack the palisade of Paponetty from three sides and the enemy hoisted the white flag as early as 10 a.m. None of the higher VOC-officers paid attention to the white flag, probably as a result of intoxication and so some VOC-soldiers were soon inside Paponetty, leading to casualties on both sides. When the enemy held up the white flag for the second time, the fighting ceased. It was agreed that the Indian soldiers of the samurin of Calicut would be allowed to leave the palisade with their muskets. When the withdrawal started around 4 pm, the Portuguese and English mercenaries – who had not been granted a free withdrawal – set the powder magazine on fire, doubtless hoping to create an escape for themselves. The result was a panic among the Indian soldiers, interpreted by many VOC-soldiers as a revolt, escalating into a massacre by the VOC-soldiers, in spite of the agreement. In total, the campaign cost the lives of some 2,000 men of the samurin of Calicut. The VOC pulled down the palisade of Paponetty and retook the fort at Siltua, thus restoring Dutch power in Malabar.

After the fierce battle of Paponetty, Hasenbosch stayed for some time in Cochin or in its vicinity. In those days Cochin consisted of a small, walled town and a fort. In fact, Cochin looked like a Batavia in miniature, although Cochin lacked the typical Dutch canal pattern. Cochin had been in Dutch hands since 1663, when the Dutch had conquered the town from the Portuguese. When Hasenbosch was in Cochin, the Catholic churches built by the Portuguese had already been pulled down, except for one that was used for Protestant services and another in use as a storehouse. As Batavia, Cochin had a complex social structure with many groups, of which the white VOC-employees were only a small minority. Not very surprisingly, the white VOC-employees in Cochin were often married with Asian or Indo-European women. Another important group consisted of Portuguese half-breeds or released slaves, in Dutch called *Toepassen*. Like the *Mardijkers* in Batavia, the *Toepassen* kept using the Portuguese language, although the Portuguese had been expelled some decades before.

In early June 1718 Hasenbosch, still in Cochin, made a remarkable decision. He cashed his complete outstanding salary, notably 75 guilders, 5 *stuivers* and 3 *penningen*[36] and donated it, via a notary in Cochin, for the building of a Lazarus house for lepers in Cochin. We can only guess why Hasenbosch made such a generous gift, with a value of more than two thirds of his annual salary. Perhaps he wanted to build up a reputation as a "model soldier", because the VOC had requested its personnel in Cochin to make some donations for the house.

In August 1720 Hasenbosch returned to Batavia, a town he had not seen for almost five years. After arrival, he was promoted to corporal, by which his monthly salary rose from 9 to 14 guilders. He was housed in the small fort of Batavia, not far from the Castle where he had spent in the beginning of his service. We have no information about his life as a corporal but the tasks of a corporal were quite clear. A corporal had to supervise the military discipline of the soldiers, such as changing the

---

[36] A Dutch guilder equalled 20 *stuivers* and a *stuiver* equalled 16 *penningen*.

guards and arranging the short leaves. A corporal also had to give corporal punishments to soldiers who had neglected their duties.

When Hasenbosch returned to Batavia in August 1720, his father Johannes and his two elder sisters, Cornelia and Ursula, were still living in that town, whereas his younger sister Maria Elizabeth had returned to the United Provinces. Regrettably, we know nothing about Hasenbosch's contacts with his family members in Batavia. However, in his new function Hasenbosch might well have had better opportunities for family visits than during his first stay in Batavia five years before. The other three family members in Batavia seem to have kept contact with one another. For example, on 5 November 1722 the first child of the second marriage of Cornelia – who had remarried after having become a widow - was baptised, with Cornelia's father and sister as official witnesses.

In 1721 or 1722 Hasenbosch was promoted further, to military clerk at the Utrecht Gate of Batavia. A "military clerk" was a sort of minor bookkeeper, with a salary of 16 guilders a month.

About 15 August 1722, Hasenbosch did something striking. He ordered to make his complete outstanding salary, with the high value of 287 guilders, 2 *stuivers* and 4 *penningen* payable to a man called Jan Backer, living in the native country. According to the preserved salary logs[37] Jan Backer cashed indeed that amount on 14 August 1723, one year after Hasenbosch's decision. In a long passage – in stately 18th century Dutch – we also read about two men functioning as proxies of Hasenbosch together with two notaries involved in the payment. In the same passage we also read that Hasenbosch had been summoned to pay a number of times during the preceding years.

Who was this "Jan Backer" and why did he claim all that money? We can only speculate. Did Hasenbosch, as a teenager in his native country, do something wrong to Jan Backer or his family? Should the payment be regarded as some settlement in civil justice? Should Hasenbosch's decision to move to Batavia, in a poorly paid job as a soldier, be regarded

---

[37] Koolbergen, *Ibid*, pp.83-85 and 250-251. In fact, the salary logs were one of the prime sources for Koolbergen to reconstruct the life of Hasenbosch.

as a flight? How did the mysterious Jan Backer find out that Hasenbosch was living in Batavia? Once again, we can only speculate.

In July 1723 Johannes Hasenbosch, the father of Leendert Hasenbosch, died in Batavia, at the age of fifty or fifty-one. From a preserved document we know that Johannes Hasenbosch died as the sexton of the "Portuguese Outer Church", a church of the official Dutch Reformed religion. At that time, Leendert Hasenbosch was still military clerk at the Utrecht Gate of Batavia.

In 1724 Hasenbosch decided to return to the United Provinces, probably to start a new career over there. Somewhere in October 1724 he went on board the *Prattenburg*, still a clerk with a monthly salary of 16 guilders but functioning as the bookkeeper of the ship (a bookkeeper had a monthly salary of 22 guilders). The *Prattenburg* left Batavia some weeks later, on 1 December 1724. The *Prattenburg* was one of the sixteen[38] ships of the return fleet under commodore Ewout van Dishoeck.

No doubt, Hasenbosch's homeward voyage on the *Prattenburg* was far more luxurious than his outward voyage and his shipments between Batavia and Cochin. As an officer, Hasenbosch probably had a private cabin on the relatively luxurious after decks. The after decks were for the officers and passengers only and were forbidden territory for the crew and soldiers. No doubt, Hasenbosch had far better and more varied meals than the crew and soldiers "before the mast". Between Batavia and Capetown, a contagious disease – possibly typhus - broke out on the *Prattenburg*, resulting in twenty deaths "before the mast" but none among the officers. On the *Prattenburg*, the number of casualties was much higher than on the other ships of the fleet[39].

Between 19 March and 11 April 1725 the *Prattenburg* made her compulsory stop at Capetown. Perhaps Hasenbosch made excursions

---

[38] Two other ships sailed from Batavia a few days later. The number of 18 ships was also mentioned in chapter 3, the chapter that describes the "detective work" of Michiel Koolbergen to find his man.

[39] Koolbergen, *Ibid* p.86 and DAS 1978/1987, *Dutch-Asiatic shipping in the 17th and 18th centuries*.

with other officers to the Table Mountain or to the vineyards of Stellenbosch.

On 11 April 1725 the *Prattenburg* left Capetown. The entire homebound fleet now consisted of twenty-three ships, including five ships that had started their voyages at Ceylon. On 17 April Hasenbosch was sentenced "to be set ashore, as a villain" on the island of Ascension, as a punishment for sodomy. The sentence was passed by the *Breede Raad* (Broad Council) of Commodore Ewout van Dishoeck and all the captains of the fleet. What happened between 11 April and 17 April 1725? Since the logs of all ships of the fleet are missing in the archives[40], we can only guess. According to Koolbergen, the most likely scenario was as follows. Hasenbosch had sex with a sailor, soldier or boy after departure from Capetown. Hasenbosch was either caught *in flagrante delicto* or was betrayed afterwards. The sailor, soldier or boy was simply thrown overboard but Hasenbosch was treated differently, because of his high rank. Koolbergen supported his scenario by pointing to other cases of sodomy judged by the VOC in those days. Even in case of a rape, the judges did not distinguish between "active" and "passive" sodomy. Both men were often punished in the same way, for instance by binding them back-to-back and throwing them overboard[41].

Personally, I do not agree with Koolbergen's statement that his scenario is the most likely one. Would the *Breede Raad* really have decided to such a horrible demonstration of class justice, which might well lead to revolt among the crew? In my opinion, other scenarios are more likely.

If Hasenbosch had indeed had sex with a boy after the departure from Capetown, there is a chance that the boy was spared or sentenced to a lesser punishment. This scenario is possible if the boy was very young[42].

---

[40] See also chapter 3. We know about the sentence from Hasenbosch's salary logs and we know about the *Breede Raad* of the commodore and captains of the fleet from the first sentence of *An Authentick Relation*, the first English version of Hasenbosch's diary on Ascension. In a VOC-convoy, serious crimes were generally dealt with by the Broad Council and not by the ship's council of a single ship.

[41] See chapter 12 for prosecution of sodomites in the United Provinces (especially the VOC) in general.

[42] See chapter 12 for details about the prosecution of adolescents.

A completely different scenario is as follows. Let us assume that Hasenbosch was drunk or boastful one day and said too much, making allusions about intimacies he had had with other men or boys, perhaps long ago. Let us assume further, that Hasenbosch's insinuations were passed on to the higher officers. Subsequently, Hasenbosch might have been arrested, interrogated and perhaps tortured, not only to make him officially confess his deeds of sodomy but also to make him reveal the names of his accomplices. Perhaps, he only mentioned names of people who were not on board or even dead. Perhaps he mentioned no names at all.

We can only guess about what happened between 11 April 1725 (departure from Capetown) and 17 April (the day of the sentence). We also know nothing about Hasenbosch's situation on board between 17 April (the day of the sentence) and 5 May (the day he was marooned). Was he perhaps in chains all the time?

On 27 April 1725, the *Prattenburg* passed the island of Saint Helena. No doubt, Hasenbosch's judges thought Saint Helena inappropriate to set him ashore, because Saint Helena was inhabited and owned by the English East India Company. On 3 May 1725 the ship reached Ascension, where Hasenbosch was left behind with a survival kit two days later. For the VOC, Leendert Hasenbosch ceased to exist.

*Clarence Bay and Long Beach, a sandy beach on Ascension (at the location of present Georgetown), looking to dark volcanic rocks to the north. The picture shows tracks made by turtles and a female Green Turtle (*Chelonia mydas*) returning to the sea after nesting. In the air we see three Ascension Frigatebirds (*Fregata aquila*). On 5 May 1725 the Dutch castaway, Leendert Hasenbosch, was almost certainly set ashore on this beach. In those days, the view was probably very similar (drawing by Anneke de Vries, from a photo by Annette Broderick, slightly adjusted).*

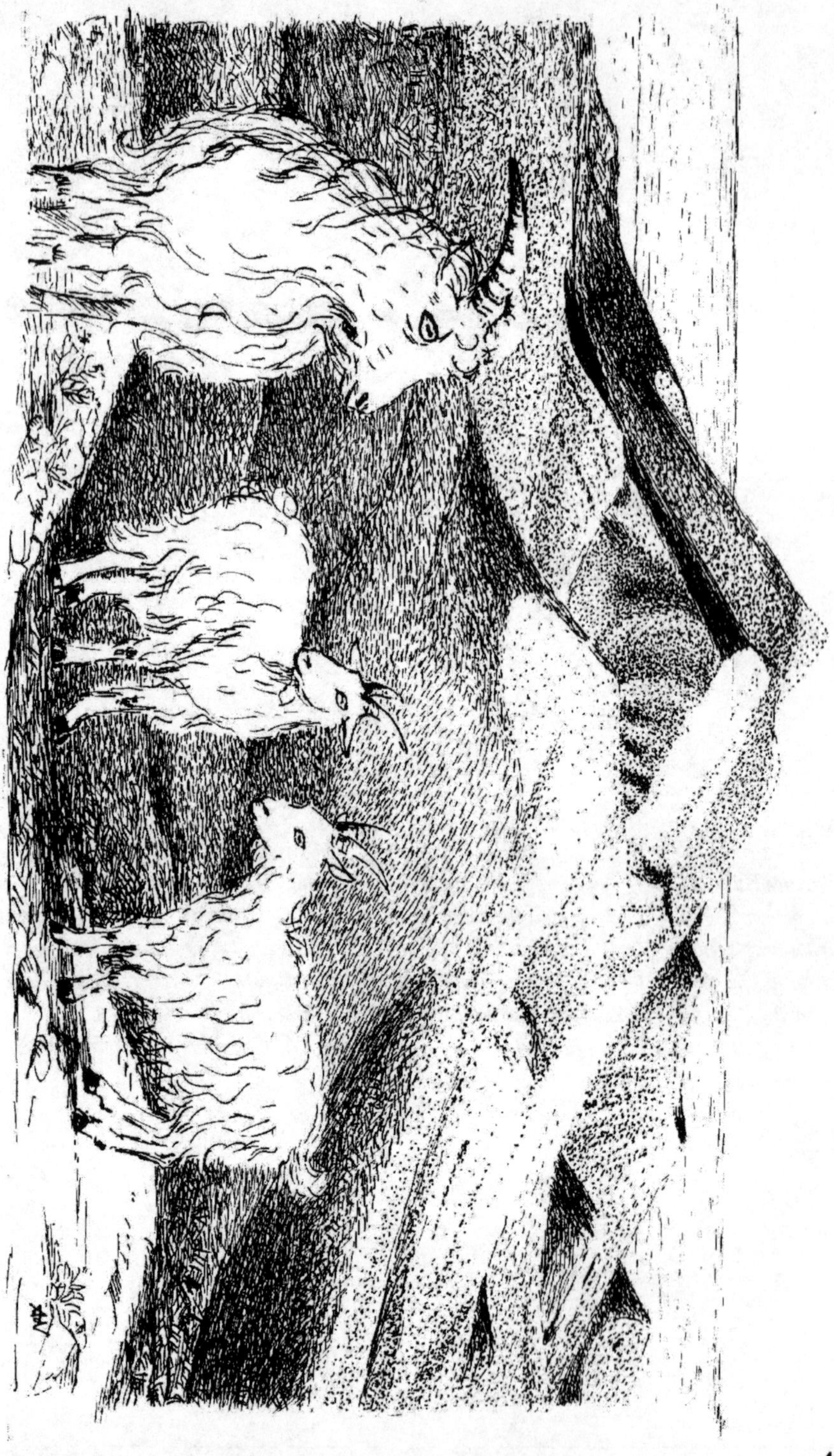

(Caption to picture on the previous page) A view over Sisters Peak and surroundings, from the western slopes of Green Mountain, as it might have looked like in 1725, with the sea horizon in background. This drawing was made by Anneke de Vries, from a photo by the author taken from Mountain Road: the lush vegetation, the road and the houses of Two Boats Village have been removed and the goats have been added. The goats were later replaced by sheep, because they were less devastating to the vegetation.

*Comfortless Cove, with Cross Hill in the background, with a Red-footed Booby (*Sula sula*) in the right and a Yellow-billed Boatswain Bird (official English name White-tailed Tropicbird (*Phaeton lepturus*)) in the left. This look is probably the same as it was in 1725 (drawing by Anneke de Vries, from three photos by the author).*

CHAPTER 5. May to October 1725: Leendert Hasenbosch on Ascension, "set ashore as a villain"

On Saturday, 5 May 1725, Leendert Hasenbosch, about thirty years of age and probably healthy, was set ashore on Ascension, at Clarence Bay, probably at Long Beach. All data about his sufferings are in the English version of his diary, published in London and Dublin in 1728 under the title *An Authentick Relation*. Unfortunately, we do not have the original diary and it is doubtful if it will ever turn up.

This chapter contains the complete text of *An Authentick Relation*. I have not modernised spelling or grammar. However, I changed the layout somewhat, by always taking a new line to mention the date. For example, the official text of *An Authentick relation* from 8 to 10 August 1725 reads:

> The 8th, 9th and 10th Ditto, searched carefully, but found no Water. Have employed my self in praying and interceding with God to have mercy on my Soul.

I decided to write in this case (and similar cases):

> **8 to 10 August 1725**
> Searched carefully, but found no Water. Have employed my self in praying and interceding with God to have mercy on my Soul.

In many cases I added annotations to the text of *An Authentick Relation*, in another font, explaining the text. The annotations marked (MK) were made by Michiel Koolbergen in his book and have been translated or rewritten by me. I agree with all annotations marked (MK), although I did not take over all Koolbergen's annotations. Annotations marked (AR) have been written by me and include some critical remarks on Koolbergen's analysis. For my annotations, I often consulted one or more of the biologists Stedson Stroud, Philip Ashmole, Myrtle Ashmole, Annette Broderick and Brendan Godley.

Saturday, 5 May 1725

By Order of the Commadore and Captains of the Dutch Fleet, I was set on Shore on the Island of Ascension, which gave me a great deal of Dissatisfaction, but I hope Almighty God will be my Protection. They put ashore with me a Cask of water, two Buckets, and an old Frying-Pan, &c. I made my Tent on the Beach near a Rock, wherein I put some of my Clothes.

> (AR) Hasenbosch was probably set ashore on Long Beach, near the main anchoring spot in those days. The "Rock" is the rock formation on the south end of Long Beach. Nowadays, there are both a fort and a landing pier at the spot of that rock formation.

6 May 1725

I went upon the Hills to see if I could discover any Thing on the other side of the Island that was more commodious for my Living, and to see if there were any Thing green; but to my great Sorrow found nothing at all worth mentioning.

I sincerely wished that some Accident would befall me, to finish these miserable Days. In the Evening I walked to my Tent again, but could not very well find the way. I walked very melancholy along the Strand, praying to God Almighty to put a Period to my Days or help me off this desolate Island. I went back to my tent, and secured it n the best I could with Stones and a Tarpaulin from the Weather. About four or five a Clock, I killed three Birds called Boobies; skinned and salted them, and put them in the Sun to dry, being the first thing I killed upon the Island. The same Night I caught two more, which I served as before.

- (MK) Under the date 6 May we see a description of activities, without a consistent chronological order. Probably Hasenbosch wrote these entries down on the morning of 7 May.
- (AR) Michiel Koolbergen thought that "the other side of the Island" was probably the north and northeast of Ascension. However, Stedson Stroud and I think that the castaway probably referred to the southwest and south, because walking to the south would have been much easier than walking to the northeast with its extensive clinker fields.

- *(MK) "walked very melancholy along the Strand"* : *Long Beach.*

- *(MK) "About four or five a Clock"*: *the afternoon of 6 May.*

- *(MK) "The same Night"*: *the night from 6 to 7 May.*

7 May 1725

In the Morning I went to my Water-Cask, it being half a League from my tent. I first put a peg in, but lost much Water by that; so got him upon his head, and took the head out with a great deal of trouble.

I made a white Flag, which I put upon my Piece, having nothing else, and set it upon a Hill near the Sea. I had no Powder or Shot, which rendered Gun useless.

That night I put more Stones about my Tent.

- *(MK) Leendert Hasenbosch was set ashore with his survival kit at Long Beach. The distance between his tent and his water-cask was definitely less than half a league, i.e. 2.4 kilometres; the translator/rewriter must have made a mistake, for in reality the distance was probably not more than about 200 metres.*

- *(MK) "That Night I put more Stones about my Tent"*: *Hasenbosch must have added this entry on 8 May, under the date 7 May.*

8 May 1725

In the Morning, I took my Flag again, and set it upon a Hill on the other side of the Island. In the way I found a Turtle, and killed him with the Butt-end of my Musket; and so went back again to my Tent, and sat me down very weary. I trust in God Almighty, that he will deliver me some time or other by some Ship that may touch here.

This Night I moved my Tent on the other side of the Rock, being afraid that it would fall on my Head, and by that means endanger my Life; I would by no means be accessory to my own Death, still hoping that God will preserve me to see better Days. On the whole Island I can't find a better Place the where I now am, and that I must me contented in my Condition. I thank God I am now in good Health.

In the Evening I killed some more Boobies, which I served as the former, and in the Morning did the same.

- *(MK) Under the date 8 May we see a description of activities, without a consistent chronological order. Probably Hasenbosch wrote all this on the morning of 9 May.*
- *(AR)* "I took my Flag again, and set it upon a Hill on the other side of the Island" : *Michiel Koolbergen thought that the castaway probably referred to the north- or northeast side of Ascension but Stedson Stroud and I think the south- and southwest sides are far more likely (see under 6 May).*
- *(MK)* "This Night I moved my Tent on the other side of the Rock" : *the night from 8 to 9 May;*
- *(MK)* "(…) the other side of the Rock" : *Hasenbosch meant the rocky structure that separated Long Beach and Deadman's Beach. Obviously, Hasenbosch moved from Long Beach to the adjoining Deadman's Beach.*

9 May 1725

In the Morning I went to look for the Turtle, which I killed yesterday. I carried my Hatchet, and cut him up on the Back, for he was so big that I could not turn him. I cut off some of the Flesh from the Fore-Finn, and brought it to my tent, to make a Bulwark of Stones round my Tent and secured it from the Weather with my Tarpaulin.

10 May 1725

In the Morning, I took four or five Onions, a few Peas and Calivances[43], and went to the south side of the Island, to see if I could find a proper Place to set them. I looked carefully on the Strand, to see if I could discover that Tracts of any Beasts, or Water, or any thing else that might be serviceable; but found nothing but a little Porcelain on the other side

---

[43] "Calivances" are chick-peas in modern English.

of the Island, which I eat for Refreshment, being very dry, and could find no Water, and but a little of it in my Sack; walking back, ate what I had before reserved. When I was halfway back, found some more Greens, but knew not whether they were good to eat.

- (AR) The south side of the island is probably the area of South West Bay and South Gannet Hill, close to what is now the airport area.
- (AR) "Porcelain" is purslane in modern English and refers to Portulaca oleracea, *the indigenous purslane of both Ascension and Saint Helena.*
- (AR, having consulted Stedson Stroud). The greens that the castaway did not dare to eat could have been small indigenous plants, which grew around the rocky beach areas, notably Euphorbia origanoides *or* Commicarpus helenae (*locally called hogweed*).

11 May 1725

In the Morning, went into the Country again, and found some Roots, the Skin somewhat resembling Potatoes, but could not think they were good to eat. I made a diligent search for a greater Discovery, but found nothing else. I sate me down very disconsolate almost dead with Thirst, and afterwards went to my Tent.

On the other side of the Island there is a sandy Bay by the biggest Hill.

This evening boiled a little Rice, being the first Time; I was somewhat out of order.

- (AR, having consulted the Ashmoles and Stedson Stroud). The plant looking like a potato could have been Ipomoea pes-caprae, *closely related to the sweet potato* Ipomoea batatus. *According to Stedson Stroud the plant could also be an endemic fern that grows from a tuber or large corme that could resemble something edible – this grows higher up the mountain.*
- (AR) "On the other side of the Island there is a sandy Bay by the biggest Hill" : Koolbergen thought that this was probably North East Bay and that Hasenbosch overlooked that area from East Crater, also called "Broken Tooth". However, Stedson Stroud and I think Mars Bay and

Shelley Beach in the south west of the island are more likely. Perhaps Hasenbosch overlooked that area from South Gannet Hill.

12 May 1725

In the Morning, boiled a little more Rice, of which I ate some. After I had prayed, I went again to the Country to see of I could discover any Ships, but to my great Sorrow saw none; so I went back again to my Tent, and then walked along the Beach, and found nothing but some Shells of Fish.

I kept constantly walking about the Island, that being all my hopes; then went to my Tent, and read till I was weary, and afterwards mended my Clothes.

This Afternoon put the Onions, Peas and Calivances in the Ground just by my Tent, to see if they would produce any more; for as it was, I could not afford Water to boil them.

(MK) "(...) and read till I was weary" : Hasenbosch possessed both a bible and a prayer's book on Ascension, as can be concluded from entries under the dates 22 May and 16 June.

13 May 1725

In the Morning, went to see if I could find any Seafowls Eggs, but found none. At my walking back, I found a small Turtle just by my Tent. I took some of its Eggs and Flesh, and boiled with my Rice for my Dinner, and buried the rest in the Sand, that it might not infect me; its Eggs I buried in the Sand likewise.

Afterwards I found some Nests of Fowls Eggs, of which I boiled in the Evening, and it was very good Diet. I melted some of the Turtles Fat to make Oil, and in the Night burnt of it, having nothing for a Lamp but a Saucer.

> *(MK) Presumably, Hasenbosch wrote down the text of "13 May" on the afternoon of 14 May, because we read "and wrote my Journal" under the date of 14 June.*

14 May 1725

In the Morning, after I had prayed, I took my usual walk, but found nothing new; so I returned again to my Tent, and sat down and mended my Banyan Coat, and wrote my Journal.

> *(MK) The last sentence is the first clear evidence that Hasenbosch was not writing in his journal every day; he probably did not describe his adventures under "13 May" until the afternoon of 14 May.*

15 May 1725

Before I took my walk, I ate some boiled Rice, and afterwards proceeded: but go nothing but my usual Game, viz. Boobies. I read till I was weary, and then betook my self to my Repose.

16 May 1725

I looked out, as the Day past; only caught no Boobies.

17 May 1725

I was very much dejected that I had found no Sustenance, and a Booby that I kept alive seven or eight Days now died.

18 May 1725

After my usual Custom of Praying, I caught two Boobies.

19 May 1725

Nothing worth of Note.

48

20 May 1725

Caught one Booby.

21 May 1725

Nothing at all.

22 May 1725

After Breakfast went to the other side of the Island, to see if I could discover any thing; but went back as I came.

At four in the Afternoon took my Line and fished on the Rock for three or four Hours, but to no purpose. I then took a melancholy Walk to my Flag; but much to my Concern could descry nothing. At my return to my tent, much to my Surprise, I found it all of a smoke. After a serious Consideration, I thought that I had left my Tinderbox a-fire on my Quilt; but the smoke smothered me so much, that could not enter before I had brought a Bucket of Water and quenched it. I return God Almighty my hearty Thanks that all my Things were not burnt. I have lost nothing by it but a Banyan Shirt, a Corner of my Quilt, and my Bible singed. I entreat God Almighty to give me the patience of holy Job to bear with my Sufferings.

- *(MK) "(…) took my Line and fished on the Rock for three or four Hours" : the "rock" was probably the rocky structure that was the border of Long Beach and Deadman's Beach. According to the time indications, this text was probably written in the late evening or at night; Hasenbosch had made himself a lamp [see under 13 May], and so he was able to write at night as well; the lamp is mentioned under the date of 20 June as well.*

- *(AR) "I then took a melancholy Walk to my Flag" : Michiel Koolbergen thought the flag was probably on the north- or northeast side of the island but Stedson Stroud and I think it was probably in the south. See also the annotations under 6 May and 8 May.*

23 May 1725

All this day was remaking what was burnt yesterday.

24 May 1725

I walked to my Flag, and returned again, with catching but one Booby. Afterwards mended my Clothes, and broiled a Booby on the Embers.

25 May 1725

After my breakfast went to my usual employment and caught several seafowls sitting on their Eggs. Ten returned home with my Spoil, and dried them. After my dinner went upon a search for more Fowls, of which I caught many, and did not forget to look out for Ships; but returned without any Discovery. Boiled some of my Eggs, and was disappointed by finding young ones in many of them.

26 May 1725

I looked out as before, but no Fowls.

27 May 1725

Nothing worthy of Note.

28 May 1725

I went to the west side of the Island along the Strand, and mounted the Precipice of a high Hill, which was so steep, that I have reason to thank God that I did not break my Neck down.

> *(AR) Michiel Koolbergen thought that Hasenbosch probably climbed Lady Hill (330 metres). Stedson Stroud and I think that Cat Hill and South Gannet Hill are more likely.*

29 May 1725

Nothing remarkable.

30 May 1725

As before.

31 May

Was forced to feed on the Provision, which I had before salted.

1 to 4 June 1725

It would be needless to write how often my Eyes are cast on the Sea to look for Shipping, and every little Atom in the Sky I take for a Sail; then look till my Eyes dazzle. And immediately the Object disappears.

When I was put on Shore, the Captain told me it was the time of the Year for Shipping to pass this way, which makes me look out the more diligently.

> *(MK) The captain was almost certainly Jan van der Heiden of the VOC-ship* Prattenburg, *on which Hasenbosch had been employed as the bookkeeper.*

5, 6 and 7 June 1725

I never neglected taking my usual Walks; but to no purpose.

8 June 1725

My Water is so much reduced, that I had but two Quarts left, and that so thick as obliged me to strain it through a Handkerchief. I then too late began to dig, and after I had dug seven Foot deep, found no moisture; the Place where I began, was in the middle of the Island. I then came back again to my Tent, but to no purpose, having digged a Fathom deep. It is impossible to express my Concern, first in not seeing any Ships to convoy me off the Island, and then in finding no Sustenance on it.

9 June 1725

Found nothing; past away the Day in Meditations on a future State.

10 June 1725

With the very last of my Water boiled some Rice; having but very little Hopes of any thing but perishing, I commended my Soul to Almighty God entreating him that he will have mercy on it, but not caring to give over all Hopes while I could yet walk.

I went to the other side of the Island to see for some water. Having heard talk there was a Well of Water on it, I walked up and down the Hills, thinking not to leave any place secret for me. After four hours tedious walking, began to grow very thirsty, and the Heat of the Sun with that made my Life a greater Burden that I was able to bear; but was resolved to proceed as long as I could stand. Walking among the Rocks, God of his great Bounty led me to a Place where some Water run out of a hollow place in the Rock. It's impossible to express my great Joy and Satisfaction in finding of it, and thought I should have drank till I burst. I sate me down for some time by it, then drank again and walked home to my Tent, having no ship to carry any along with me.

> *(MK) The place* "where some Water run out of a hollow place in the Rock" *must have been the place nowadays called Dampier's Drip, at the foot of Green Mountain [to the northwest of that mountain].*

11 June 1725

In the morning, after I had returned God Almighty my hearty Thanks, I took my Tea Kettle with some Rice in it and some Wood along with me to the Place where the Water was, and there boiled and ate it.

12 June 1725

I boiled some Rice to break my Fast, and afterwards with much trouble carried two Buckets of Water to my tent. I often think I am possessed with Things that I really want; but when I come to search, find it only a Shadow.

My shoes being worn out, the Rocks cut my feet to pieces; and I am often afraid of tumbling, and by that means endanger the breaking of my Buckets, which I can't be without.

> *(AR) This is the only entry about shoes in the diary. Hasenbosch probably only had one pair of shoes.*

13 June 1725

I went to look out for Wood, but found non but a little Weeds somewhat like Birch; brought it to my Tent, and boiled some of it for my Dinner. Afterwards went and looked out for Shipping, but to no purpose. It makes me very melancholy to think that have no Hopes of getting off this unhappy Island.

> *(AR, having consulted the Ashmoles and Stedson Stroud). The plant or tree looking like birch might have been the extinct shrub* Oldenlandia adscensionis, *which also may have been seen by William Dampier in 1701.*

*A Brown Booby (*Sula leucogaster*). As they can be caught easily, boobies were popular food for mariners - and the Dutch castaway - in past times (drawing by Anneke de Vries, from a photo by the author).*

14 June 1725

Took my Tea Kettle with some Rice, and went into the Country where the Water was. Afterwards returned again to my Tent, and mended my Clothes, and past away the rest of the Day in reading.

> *(MK) Obviously, Hasenbosch walked to Dampier's Drip, to have his meal of rice over there.*

15 June 1725

All the Day employed in getting Seafowls Eggs and Birch.

16 June 1725

To no purpose looked for Ships; and in the Night was surprised by a Noise round my Tent of Cursing and Swearing, and the most blasphemous Conversations that I ever heard. My Concern was so great, that I thought I should have died with the Fright. I did nothing but offer up my Prayers to the Almighty to protect me in this miserable Circumstance; but my fright rendered me in a very bad Condition of praying, I trembling to that degree, that I could not compose my Thoughts; and any body would have believed that the Devil had moved his Quarters, and was coming to keep Hell on Ascension. I was certain that there was no human Creature on the Island but myself, having not seen the Footsteps of any man but my own; and so much libidinous Talk was impossible to be expressed by any body but Devils. And to my greater Surprise I was certain that I was very well acquainted with one of the Voiced, it bearing a affinity of an intimate Acquaintance of mine; and I really thought that I was sometimes touched by an invisible Spirit. I made my application to the Father, Son and Holy Ghost for forgiveness of my Sins, and that they would protect me from these evil Spirits. It was three a Clock in the Morning before they ceased tormenting me, and then being very weary, I fell to sleep. In the Morning I awoke about seven a-clock and returned God Almighty my hearty and sincere Thanks for his last Night's Protection of me, but still heard some Shrieks near my Tent, but could see nothing. I took my Prayer Book, and read the Prayers proper for a Man in my Condition, and at the same time heard a Voice, crying, Bouger. I can't afford paper enough to set down every particular of this unhappy Day.

- *(AR) This text will be examined in detail in chapter 9, where it will be stated that the remarks about devils and "Footsteps of any man but my own" are in the writing style of Daniel Defoe, who might well have been the English translator/rewriter of the diary. It is not impossible that parts of the text under this date were written by Hasenbosch himself and were "enhanced" by the English translator/rewriter. If Hasenbosch himself wrote parts of the text, we might think that Hasenbosch suffered from hallucinations partly created by crying seabirds around his tent. Stedson Stroud made two useful suggestions: Hasenbosch might have had hallucinations from both drinking boil weeds and from scurvy. He might have had a touch of scurvy from eating much salted meats.*

- *(MK)* "(…) I was certain that I was very well acquainted with one of the Voices, it bearing a affinity of an intimate Acquaintance of mine; and I really thought that I was sometimes touched by an invisible Spirit": *this acquaintance is described again under the date of 20 June as the ghost of a deceased friend, who was a soldier at Batavia.*

- *(AR) The modern spelling for "bouger" is "bugger".*

White Tern (Gygys alba), one of the noisy bird species that the castaway must have heard very often (drawing by Anneke de Vries, from a photo by Stedson Stroud).

17 June 1725

I fetched home two Buckets of Water and dreaded Night's coming on, and interceded with God Almighty that I might not be troubled again with those evil Spirits; and I hope God Almighty heard my Prayers, for I was not perplexed with them this Night.

Before I came upon this miserable island, I was of the Protestant religion, and used to laugh at the Romans when they talked to me of Apparitions; but to my great Sorrow now find smarting Reasons to the contrary, and shall henceforth embrace their Opinions.

This Day an Apparition appeared to me in the similitude of a Man, whom I perfectly knew; he conversed with me like a Human Creature, and touched me so sensibly of the Sins of my past Life (of which I have a sincere and hearty Repentance) and was such a terrible Shock to me, that I wished it would kill me.

- *(MK) "I fetched home two Buckets of Water" : obviously, Hasenbosch went to Dampier's Drip once again.*
- *(AR) Some entries under this date (and other dates) refer to a guilty conscience, evil spirits and apparitions. Personally, I think Hasenbosch did not write so much about those matters. In my view, it is more likely that the majority of those entries were invented by the English translator/rewriter, to make the story more interesting.*

18 June 1725

After my Devotions went to look out, and carried my Hatchet with me. On the Strand, the other Side of the Island, I found a Tree, which I believe Providence had cast ashore for me. I cut it in two Pieces, the whole being to big for me to carry. I put one half on my Shoulders, and when I was half way home, set it down and rested my self on it. During which time, the Apparition appeared to me again; his Name I am afraid to utter, fearing the Event. He haunts me so often, that I begin to grow accustomed to him. After I had rested my self, I carried it home and then went back and fetched the other half.

(AR) Michiel Koolbergen thought that "the other side of the island" was the northeast but Stedson Stroud and I think of the southwest.

19 June 1725

In the Morning went to my Colours to see if I could discover any Ships. Last Night nor this Day I have not seen any thing, and I trust in God I shall be no more troubled with them.

20 June 1725

This night, contrary to my expectation, was so prodigiously perplexed with Spirits, and tumbled up and down in my tent to that degree, that in the Morning my Flesh was like a Mummy; and the Person that I was formerly acquainted with spoke to me several times this Night: but I can't think he would do any harm, for when he was in this World we were as great as two own brothers. He was a Soldier at Batavia.

It is impossible for a Man to survive so many Misfortunes, I not being able to keep a Light; but the Saucer that contains it, is jumbled about and broke: and, if God of his Infinite Goodness does not help me, I must inevitably perish. I hope this my Punishment in this World may suffice for my most heinous Crime of making use of my Fellow-Creature to satisfy my Lust, whom the Almighty Creator had ordained another Sex for. I only desire to live to make atonement for my Sins, which I believe my Comrade is damned for.

I spent all the Day in Meditations and Prayers, and ate nothing. My strength decays, and my Life is become a great Burthen to me.

- *(MK)* "(....) contrary to my expectation" : *the expectation written under the date of 19 June.*
- *(MK)* "(...) and the Person that I was formerly acquainted with spoke to me several times this Night" : *this person was first mentioned under the date of 16 June.*

- *(AR) "He was a soldier at Batavia" : Hasenbosch had had a military career at Batavia himself, so this entry might refer to a homosexual relationship.*

- *(MK) "I not being able to keep a Light ; but the Saucer that contains it, is jumbled about and broke" : Hasenbosch used a saucer with melted fat of a turtle as a lamp, created on 13 May*

21 June 1725

In the Morning, I lifted up my Hands to Heaven, and offered up all my Prayers, and then went to my Flag; and in the way looked for Provisions to assuage my raging Hunger, but found none, so was forced to be satisfied with salted Fowls.

22 June 1725

My Water being expended, took my Bucket and went for more: but the way was so troublesome and the Rocks so sharp to my bare Feet, that it took me best part of the Day to bring it home. And in the Afternoon I went to the proper Place for Fowls Eggs, of which I found some; they were speckled like some of our Holland's Bird Eggs.

(MK) Obviously, Hasenbosch went once again to Dampier's Drip to get more water. Hasenbosch's "speckled eggs" probably refer to the eggs of the Sooty Tern (Sterna fuscata), called Wideawake Tern by the people living on Ascension nowadays.

23 June 1725

Looked out for Ships and passed away the rest of the Day in Prayers.

24 to 27 June 1725

I never neglected looking out for Ships, and Victuals; then read and prayed and humbled my self before God, and desired that he would have mercy on me and deliver me off this miserable island.

Afterwards came and took my Bedding and some other Necessaries, and went to the middle of the Island, where I fixed a new Habitation in a concave place of a Rock, it being much nearer the Water than the other place. The other Day got two Days of water out of this same place, but now there is not a Drop here.

I fetched a few eggs and boiled them in my Teakettle; and went to the south side of the Island, where there is a large Hill of Sand, and a Hill of Rocks where I found some more Porcelain and some Eggs, which I gathered up and put it in my Sack. I fried both together and ate them with a good Appetite.

Upon the Strand I found a Brush, and returned, fearing I should be benighted, and not be able to find my new Abode in the Rocks. Before I got there, I was almost famished with Thirst, and my Skin blistered with the violent Heart of the Sun.

- *(MK) Obviously, Hasenbosch moved his camp to the cave nowadays called Dampier's Cave, situated in the middle of the island [near Middleton's Ridge], not far from Dampier's Drip. Almost certainly, Hasenbosch moved to this cave before 27 June, probably on 25 or 26 June; on the day of the move itself Hasenbosch probably did not have time to write entries. From the opening of Dampier's Cave, Hasenbosch could see – between the tops of the hills – in the direction of North East Bay, where he could see the sea; so that he could see a ship approaching the island.*

- *(MK) "(...) and went to the south side of the Island, where there is a large Hill of Sand, and a Hill of Rocks (...)" : possibly Mountain Red Hill and Spoon Crater; this trip took place in the morning of 27 June.*

- *(MK) "Upon the Strand" : very likely Long Beach or Deadman's Beach, where Hasenbosch's tent still was; this trip took place in the afternoon of 27 June.*

28 and 29 June 1725

I went upon the Hills, and to no purpose looked out for Ships. Afterwards walking on the Strand, I discovered a piece of Wood sticking in the Strand, which I at first took for a Tree, but when I came to it I found it was a cross. I embraced it in my Arms, and prayed to God

Almighty to deliver me: I believe there was a man buried there from some Ship.

I returned with much trouble to my Cave in the Rock, and coming down a Hill, my feet were so sore with the Rocks, that I thought I should have broke my Neck. When I got home I reposed my self a little, and then walked out again, and found a piece of broken Glass Bottle.

Afterwards found a deep Pit in the Sand, which I descended into, thinking there might be Water in it. I raked the Sand about a Foot deeper than it was before, and found some brackish Water, so that my trouble was all in vain.

Afterwards when I was rambling up and down I found some scattered Wood, which I made up in a Bundle, and bringing it home to my cave heard a Noise as if there had been Coppersmiths at Work.

Afterwards I went again to the Strand, where I got some Greens and Eggs, which I ate with Bread, and drank the Water I had left in my Cave.

- *(AR) Hasenbosch probably summarised his adventures of 28 June and 29 June under the date of 29 June, because we read about three walks, probably too much for one day. The text contains some indications from which we might presume that Hasenbosch suffered from both fever and sunstroke.*
- *(AR) In one entry we read that Hasenbosch ate bread. This must have been either a joke of Hasenbosch or a mistake of the English translator/rewriter, because Hasenbosch did not have ingredients to make bread. The descriptions of his walks are extremely vague, but if Hasenbosch found a cross on some beach indeed, then the beach was probably not Long Beach or Deadman's Beach, because he had surveyed those beaches already. Michiel Koolbergen thought of North East Bay but Stedson Stroud and I think of Comfortless Cove, because from Dampier's Cave it is much easier to walk to Comfortless Cove than to North East Bay.*
- *(AR) "a Noise as if there had been Coppersmiths at Work" : possibly, Hasenbosch heard the shrieks of hundreds of birds.*

- *(AR) "Afterwards I went again to the Strand, where I got some Greens" : "greens" might stand for purslane but Stedson Stroud has a strong feeling it might have been the indigenous plant New Zealand spinach (Tetragonia tegragonoides).*

30 June 1725

June the 30th, Here has been so much dry Weather, to my Sorrow, that both at he Cave and the other place, where there used to be water enough, there is now not one Drop, and I am as much in want of it, as I have been since my coming to this miserable Island.

- *(MK) "(...) place, where there used to be Water enough" : Dampier's Drip.*
- *(MK) From his first day, 5 May, Hasenbosch used his water sparingly. The amount of water he had received on 5 May – as part of his survival kit – had gone on 10 June. Afterwards Hasenbosch used the water of Dampier's Drip but this source (in fact a reservoir of rain water, enclosed in a layer of clay) got dry on 27 June; on 26 June he had taken out a small amount of water from Dampier's drip and stored it in one of his two buckets. However, this last amount was gone on 30 June.*

1 July 1725

The Water was dried up in ever Place where I used before to get it, so that I was near dead with Thirst.

2 July 1725

I offered up my Prayers to God to deliver me, as he had a foretime done Moses and the Children of Israel, by causing Water to flow out of a Rock. But that none of my own Endeavours might be wanting, I went to make a diligent Search, and in the way saw a matter of fifty Goats upon a Hill, and afterwards about twenty or thirty more. I pursued them with the utmost of my Ability, but they were too swift for me, and I looked carefully where they were for Water, believing that there might be some there; and I found a deep Pit, being five or six Fathoms to the Bottom, which I descended, but is was quite dry. I suppose in the Rains there is Water here, by the Goats coming to it now.

- *(MK) Hasenbosch mentions the presence of goats for the first time, 56 (!) days after he was set ashore on Ascension. Under the date of 3 July he gives an explanation for not having seen these animals before.*

- *(MK) "(...) and in the way saw a matter of fifty Goats upon a Hill"* : *probably on and near Devil's Cauldron; this can be concluded from the following statement:* "I looked carefully where they were for Water, believing that there might be some there; and I found a deep Pit, being five or six Fathoms to the Bottom (...)", *which is almost certainly referring to Goat Hole, a deep ravine to the northwest at the foot of Devil's Cauldron, about one kilometre from Dampier's Cave.*

3 July 1725

I prayed earnestly, and afterwards went to look for Water. It's a great Wonder to me how the Goats do to live in the dry seasons, seeing that water is so scarce now. I should have been famished before this time, had it not been for a reserve of about a Gallon of Water which I had before put up, thinking not to expend it till the last Necessity; but now was forced to drink of it to assuage my extreme Thirst.

I afterwards went to the Strand, but discovered nothing of service to me.

Then walked to the Country a different way from any I had been yet. Upon a Hill I saw, I am sure, at least three or four hundred Goats great and small, which I run after, but they were too nimble for me. It's surprising to me, seeing that there are so many Goats upon the Island, that I should discover more before: but I believe they skulk in the Rocks, and when Water is dried up, they come abroad for more.

I found two Gallons of Water in a place of a Rock.

- *(MK) "(...) a reserve of about a gallon of Water (...)"* : *this reserve of water had not been mentioned before. We do not know where Hasenbosch held this reserve but it was probably not far from Dampier's Cave.*

- *(MK) "(…) afterwards went to the Strand (…)"* : *probably Long Beach or Deadman's Beach.*

- *(MK) Hasenbosch gives a plausible explanation for the fact, that he did not see goats before. Most likely, the goats spent most of their time Breakneck Valley. This valley, which was not easy to access, is between the two tops of Green Mountain. In this valley, there is a water well, discovered by William Dampier in 1701; Hasenbosch, during his stay, never found this well; obviously, around 2 July this well had become dry as a result of extreme heat, and so the goats started seeking water elsewhere.*

- *(MK) "I found two Gallons of water in a place of a Rock"* : *this seems an unlikely large quantity of water. It is not impossible the translator/rewriter made a mistake by recalculating the volume written down by Hasenbosch – also because the translator/rewriter made a definite mistake in the recalculation of volumes under the date of 17 August (see under that date). Most likely, Hasenbosch found this new quantity of water (once again, probably less than two gallons) by following the goats.*

4 July 1725

I moved my Things from the Cave, and went to another part of the Island to settle my Abode, being sure that there was no Water on this side of the Island. I prayed to God, and then searched for Water, but to no purpose.

> *(MK) Obviously, Hasenbosch moved to a new abode. Unfortunately, he did not describe the location of this new abode. However, from an entry under 19 May we may conclude that it was once again a cave, a cave closer to the shoreline that Dampier's Cave; possibly it was the cave or lava tunnel close to South West Bay, in the slope of Command Hill.*

5 to 8 July 1725

I delayed no time to look for Water, unless when I prayed.

9 July 1725

As I walked upon the Strand, I heard again a very dismal Noise of Cursing and Swearing in my own Language, During the time of this Noise, I never in all my life saw so many Fowls together, they looking like a Cloud, and intercepting between me and the Sky deprived me of some of its Light.

- *(AR) Interestingly, the narrator did NOT describe a connection between his observation of "Noise of Cursing and Swearing in my own Language" and his observation of a large flock of birds; he only wrote that the two observations occurred during the same period. If Hasenbosch himself wrote the text, we might think that Hasenbosch suffered from hallucinations partly created by crying seabirds, as described in the annotations under 16 June[44].*
- *(MK) "As I walked upon the Strand" : probably Long Beach and/or Deadman's Beach. Hasenbosch often returned to this spot, as it was the prime anchoring spot as well as the spot of his tent.*

10 July 1725

I went upon a very steep Hill to look for Shipping, but see none. Upon the Hill, I found a piece of Wood which I brought down along with me to prop up my new Habitation; and coming down again, found another piece, which I brought down likewise.

- *(MK) The steep hill was possibly Sisters Peak, 446 metres.*
- *(MK) We do not know where his new habitation was but a hypothesis is given under 4 July.*

---

[44] In my view, Hart-Davis, in *Ascension, the story of a South Atlantic island*, p.21 was right when he wrote about the diary entry of 9 July 1725: "For this visitation at least there is a rational explanation. Clearly the birds were wideawake or sooty terns, which still frequent Ascension in enormous numbers, and do indeed darken the sky with their dense flocks. It is not hard to imagine how fiendish their shrill, raucous clamour must have sounded to someone half-deranged by fear, exhaustion and thirst" .

11 July 1725

I carried all the Wood from my Tent into the Country, and likewise some of my Clothes.

> *(MK) Hasenbosch's tent was still on Deadman's Beach and he carried the wood [that he needed for cooking] to his new habitation in the "country", possibly the cave close to South West Bay; see under 4 July.*

12 to 15 July 1725

Looked for Water, but found none.

16 July 1725

Found some Fowls Eggs, which I brought home to eat; used my Water very sparingly.

17 July 1725

Nothing.

18 July 1725

As before.

19 July 1725

Nothing Remarkable.

20 July 1725

Nothing worthy of Note.

21 July 1725

Having no Hopes of any thing but perishing, I committed my Soul to God, praying that he will have mercy on it. Have now very little Hopes of Shipping: I boiled some Rice and Eggs.

22 to 31 July 1725

My Heart is so full that my Pen can't utter it. I now and then find a little Water which the Goats have left for me; I always scoop it up to the last Drop, and use it very sparingly.

1 to 3 August 1725

Walked out with my Bucket in my hand, and found a very little Water, which I brought home.

4 August 1725

I found some Water in a hollow place of a rock, and rolled my Cask there, and scooped it all out as clean as I could: this rejoiced me very much.

I then walked along the Strand, and found a piece of broken Oar. Afterwards found three or four short thick pieces of Wood like Billets, and a little farther saw somewhat like a House, and having before heard that the Portuguese formerly inhabited the Island, made me go to it, to see what it was; but found only a white hollow Rock, and in the Concavity there were some Nails and broken Glass Bottles. This was of very little use to me, so took my Bundle of Wood and marched home.

- *(MK) "(...) rolled my Cask there" : the cask was still on Long Beach; the spot where Hasenbosch found water "in the place of a Rock" on 3 August, must have been somewhere on or near Long Beach or Deadman's Beach; so, Hasenbosch had two small amounts of water in two places, in his cask on the beach, and in his bucket in his cave [see under 3 August].*

- *(MK) "(...) walked along the Strand, and found a piece of broaken Oar (...)" : obviously a stretch of beach where he had not been before, because before 4 August he had – in describing his beach walks- never mentioned the presence of a white rock that looked like a house from a distance.*

5 August 1725

Nothing remarkable.

6 August 1725

Went to my Tent on the Beach, and saw three or four of the Peas and Calivances which I before set in the Ground were come up: which was at first a great Satisfaction to me, but when I looked nearer, found that the Vermin had eaten all the rest, which soon palled my former Joy.

I return God Almighty my hearty Thanks that he has thus long preserved me.

> *(AR, having consulted the Ashmoles and Stedson Stroud) The tent of Hasenbosch was still at Deadman's Beach, where he had put the peas and calivances (chickpeas) in the ground on 12 May. The "vermin" could have been rats, mice, land crabs or geckos, all of which would have found peas to be a tasty meal!*

7 August 1725

These three Months there has not been above half an Hour's Rain upon the Island, and I can't find a Drop of Water more upon the Island than what is now in my Cask: and if God Almighty of his great Goodness does not send Rain to replenish my small Stock, I must inevitably perish.

> *(MK) Obviously, the small amount of water that Hasenbosch kept in a bucket in his cave (possibly near South West Bay) had evaporated.*

8 to 10 August 1725

Searched carefully, but found no Water. Have employed my self in praying and interceding with God to have mercy on my Soul.

11 August 1725

Went to my Tent on the Strand, and again heard such a terrible Noise as if there had been a hundred Coppersmiths at Work. I was resolved to go upon the Hill to see if I could discover any Thing; and saw a Cloud of Birds, which I believe made the Noise that just now surprised me. It was a great Satisfaction to me, only to think that I was so deceived.

- *(MK) "Went to my Tent on the Strand"* ; *on Deadman's Beach.*
- *(MK) "(…) again heard such a terrible Noise as if there had been a hundred Coppersmiths at Work."* On 29 June Hasenbosch made a similar remark, see under that date.
- *(MK) "I was resolved to go upon the Hill (…)";* possibly Cross Hill.

12 to 17 August 1725

Went about every part of the Island to look for water; but to my great Concern found none; and I gauged my Cask that I had, and found there was not above six Gallons remaining, which made me boil nothing, and drink very sparingly.

- *(MK) "(…) and found there was not above six Gallons remaining (…)"* : this must be a mistake by the English translator/rewriter, because with six gallons (or 27 litres), Hasenbosch could have survived a whole extra month; under the date 25 August, eight days later, he says he drank his last amount of water, meaning that he consumed more than three litres a day during those eight days which is unlikely; he wrote under the date of 17 August of the need to use the water very sparingly; by reading the entries from 18 to 25 August, we should also conclude that the "six Gallons" mentioned in An Authentick Relation must be far too high.

18 and 19 August 1725

Could find no Water, and was out late of my Search, so that the Sun set when I was on the contrary side of the Island from my Cave, and could not find my way home; so was forced to sleep between two Rocks, and there was such a quantity of Rats there, that I thought they would eat me. I wished twenty times that I were on the Sand on the Beach.

- *(AR) Hasenbosch obviously spent the night from 18 to 19 August in the open air. If his home was indeed the cave or lava tunnel close to South West Bay, in the slope of Command Hill (see under 4 July), we must presume that Hasenbosch had ventured far into the east or northeast of the island.*

- *(AR) This is the only entry in the diary about rats. If there had been many rats near his abodes, Hasenbosch would probably have written more entries about rats. This could mean that there were few rats in the areas where Hasenbosch had his abodes. Rats probably came to the island in 1701, with the shipwreck of the Roebuck under William Dampier. Today the only species of rat on Ascension is the Black Rat (Rattus rattus).*

20 August 1725

Not a Drop of Water to be found. I Prayed to God that he would send Rain, and took my Spade and dug a well two fathoms deep, but to no purpose. I then looked up to the Heavens all round me, to see if I could see the Sky overcast, that might give me some Hopes of Rain; but all, to my Sorrow, was very clear.

(MK) Under this date, we read for the first time about a spade. A spade was not even mentioned in earlier lines about digging. Perhaps Hasenbosch made this spade himself shortly before 20 August.

21 August 1725

Went rambling about the Island with my Scoop with me to look for Water, but could not find the least Drop, and my Water almost gone at home; and was so prodigious dry, that I was forced to make water in my Scoop and drink it, thinking it was better than Salt Water, being so extreme thirsty, that my Lips were glowed together.

- *(MK) "and my Water almost gone at home" : it is very likely, that "home" was now again – just as in the month of May – Deadman's Beach or Long Beach, where the water cask was. From an entry under the date of 23 August we can also conclude that "home" was there.*
- *(AR) "make water" is an euphemism for urination.*

22 August 1725

After my Prayers went again to look for Water, and on the Strand I found a Turtle which I killed and drank near a Gallon of his Blood. I took some of its Eggs and Fat, and fried them. Its Blood and my own

Water did not contribute so much to abating my Thirst: for all I had drank near a Gallon if the Turtle's Blood, was forced again to drink my own Water.

- *(AR)* "my own Water"; *a nickname for his own urine.*
- *(AR after having consulted Brendan Godley and Annette Broderick). The turtle must have been on Deadman's Beach or Long Beach. A turtle does indeed contain about a gallon of blood.*

23 August 1725

No Hopes of finding any Water, and I took some of the Blood of the Turtle which I killed yesterday after it had settled all Night, and my own Water together, and boiled with some Tea in it. It was somewhat better than raw Blood.

At four in the Afternoon all the fresh water that I had left in the World I put in my Te-Kettle, to bring it down to my tent: shall be forced to live there now, to be near the Turtles, having nothing else to subsist on.

But was taken so violently with the Flux, drinking the Turtle's Blood, that I could not walk three Steps. I can't say but I was glad of it, hoping that it will put an end on my Misery and days at once. With a great deal of Trouble I got to my Tent by dark.

- *(AR)* "my own Water": *Hasenbosch's own urine.*
- *(AR) The remarks about turtles in the month of August are strange, because the "normal" season is from December to June, nowadays. However, it is not possible that in 1725 there were so many more turtles that there was a steady stream of turtles all over the year. Moreover, Stedson Stroud told me that even nowadays turtles are seen - occasionally and in very low numbers - outside the "normal" season.*

24 August 1725

I was still much troubled with the Flux, but was to bottle some Tea of the former Ingredients.

25 August 1725

I was so dry and sick together, that I drank my very last Water, being but a Pint. Afterwards I went to look for Fowl Eggs, to see if they would quench my extreme Thirst.

26 and 27 August 1725

I thought of little else but Death, and prayed earnestly for admittance to Heaven. The Fowls Eggs had no Effect, so was forced again to boil Tea of my urine and settled Blood, there being plenty of Turtles on the Island.

28 August 1725

At three in the Morning went out to catch a Turtle, and found one, which I killed with my Hatchet, and filled a Bucket with his Blood: he had likewise a great deal of water in his Bladder, which I drank all out, and was much better than his Blood: but it soon rose in my Stomach, and I cast it up again. I cut off some of its Flesh, and carried it to my Tent. Afterwards being very dry, I boiled some tea; but my Stomach being weak, it required somewhat more nourishing; and this was very bitter, and I soon brought it up again. I boiled more, and let it stand.

- *(MK)* "and this was very bitter" : *a mixture of urine and blood of turtles, as he drank before (see under 23, 24 and 27 August)*
- *(MK)* "I boiled more [tea], and let it stand" : *probably to let it settle down.*

29 August 1725

I could not sleep all Night, being so dry, and my Head grows dizzy, that I thought I should have run mad. I went again and searched in all Pits, but found them dry; the deepest of them, I dug seven Foot deeper, but at last found moisture.

(AR) "(...) and searched in all Pits" : *Hasenbosch seems to have dug pits at various spots, hoping to find fluids.*

30 August 1725

I prayed very earnestly most part of the day, and then laid down in my Tent, and wished that it would rain, or that I should die before I rose.

In the Afternoon got out of my tent, but was so weak that I could not walk. I was forced to take some of the eggs of the Turtle that I killed two days past, not finding one now, and ate of them. The Flesh stunk, but the Eggs did not: my Head was swelled, and so dizzy, that I knew not what I did. But I was in such agony with Thirst, that it's impossible for any body to express it. I could not see any Turtles, so caught five Boobies, and drank the Blood of them.

31 August 1725

I was walking, or, more properly speaking, crawling at the Sand, for I could not walk three Steps together. I saw a living Turtle. I was not able to carry with my Bucket, but cut off his head with my Razor, and lay all along and sucked his Blood as it ran out; and afterwards got my hands into him, and got out the Bladder, which I carried home with me, and put the water out into my Kettle. Afterwards I took my Hatchet, and went to cut him up, to get its eggs; and in cutting the Shell broke the Helve of it. This was still an Addition to my Misfortunes, but I got out some of its Eggs, and carried them home, and fried them, and afterwards drank some boiled Piss mixed with Tea; which, though it was not very nauseous, revived my very much. I made a Virtue of Necessity, and in my deplorable Condition thought it good.

1 September 1725

I killed another Turtle, but never was any poor Creature so mangled, having broke my Hatchet, and raking among his Entrails, broke the Gall; which made the Blood so bitter, that after I had boiled it, I could hardly drink it, but was forced to get it down.

I thought of nothing but the other World, and soon brought up again what I had before drank; and was so extreme dry, that I drank a quart of salt water, but could not contain it. I was so very ill after it, that I expected immediate death, and prepared my self in the best manner I could for it; and I hope the lord will have mercy on my Soul.

After it was dark, I saw a Turtle crawling towards my Tent, which I killed, and drank about two Quarts of his Blood; all the rest that I could catch, I reserved, and the endeavoured to go to sleep.

- *(MK)* "and raking among his Entrails" : *presumably, Hasenbosch was searching for the turtle's bladder, as he had done on 31 August.*
- *(AR) All the entries about the butchering of the turtles (1 September and earlier dates) look plausible, so the biologists Brendan Godley and Annette Broderick told me (except for the fact that turtles in August and September are rare nowadays). So, my guess is that the "butchering" entries were written by Hasenbosch himself and were not imagined by the English translator/rewriter.*

2 and 3 September 1725

All the Day was employed in fixing a Helve to my Hatchet. I was somehow better than yesterday, and lived upon the Turtle I killed last Night.

4 September 1725

Drank the last of the Blood, which was well settled, and a little sour.

5 to 8 September 1725

I lived upon Turtles Blood and Eggs; that my Strength decays so, that it will be impossible I should live long. I resign my self wholly to Providence, being hardly able to kill a Turtle.

9 to 11 September 1725

I am so much decayed, that I am a perfect Skeleton, and can't write the Particulars, my Hand shakes so.

12 to 17 September 1725

Lived as before. I'm in a declining Condition.

18 September to 6 October 1725

All as before.

7 October 1725

My Wood's all gone, so that I am forced to eat raw Flesh and salted fowls. I can't live long, and I hope the Lord will have mercy on my Soul.

8 October 1725

Drank my own Urine, and eat raw Flesh.

9 October to 14 October 1725

All as before.

FINIS[45]

---

[45] The London edition of 1728 ends with only "Finis". The Dublin edition of the same year ends with: "N.B. It may be justly supposed he died the above 14th of October, no Account of his Transactions being specified after that Day in his Journal found by the Sailors, as mentioned in the Title Page" (Koolbergen, *Ibid*, p.256). For details about both editions of *An Authentick Relation* see Chapter 9.

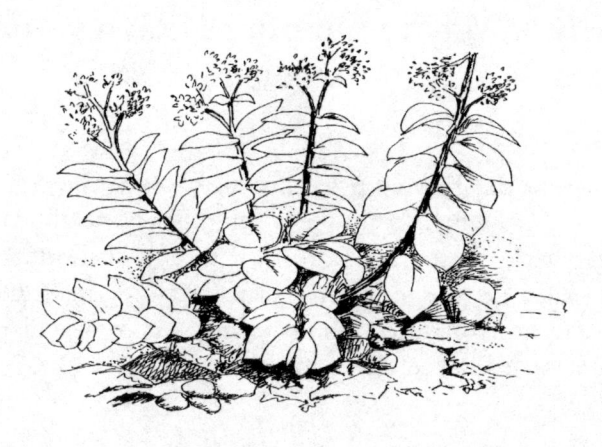

*Grazed spurge (*Euphorbia origanoides*), an example of the scarce vegetation that Ascension had in 1725 (drawing by Anneke de Vries, from a photo by Stedson Stroud).*

*Wideawake Terns, official English name Sooty Terns (*Sterna fuscata*). Nowadays this is the only seabird species breeding in huge numbers on the main island; the cats can't exterminate this species because they are away from the island for two months a year (drawing by Anneke de Vries, from a photo by Stedson Stroud).*

CHAPTER 6. May to October 1725: a summary of the castaway's stay on Ascension

Hasenbosch wrote the first entry of his diary on 5 May 1725, the very first day of his marooning. In the beginning, he wrote almost every day but after some weeks the entries become scarcer and shorter. We should keep in mind that he was not on Ascension to write some novel or tourist guide. He probably used his diary as a sort of calendar and wrote some scattered entries to keep his mind clear.

The marooning of Hasenbosch should not be regarded as a virtual death sentence, because his judges granted him a survival kit with water, food and other useful things, as we can read in various entries of *An Authentick Relation*. Most importantly, Hasenbosch was set ashore with a cask of water. We do not know the exact amount of water but it was sufficient for a few weeks, during which he had to search for water sources on the island. As to food, the survival kit included unknown quantities of onions, peas, chickpeas and rice. Hasenbosch also had a tent, bedding, clothes, a hatchet, two buckets, a teakettle, a tarpaulin, an old frying pan, a razor and a tinderbox[46]. The survival kit also included a fire weapon, probably some fowling piece or musket, which was of little use, because the kit did not include gunpowder or bullets. Hasenbosch also had some books, including at least one bible and one prayer book. Of course, he also had paper, pen and ink, otherwise he could not have written the diary[47].

Hasenbosch had been told two hopeful things prior to his marooning. Firstly, his captain had told him that it was the season during which ships passed the island. Secondly, he had been informed about a source of

---

[46] Interestingly, Captain William Mawson of the British East India Man *Compton*, whose crew found the belongings of the Dutch castaway in the end of January 1726, also mentioned "nails" among the possessions of the mysterious Dutchman. Perhaps those nails had not been included in the survival kit but were found later by Hasenbosch, on 4 August 1725. More about the discovery of the diary can be found in chapter 7.

[47] Interestingly, the diary does not mention the usual *chest* that Hasenbosch, like any employee of the VOC, must have possessed. In their logs, the two British captains whose crews found the castaway's things in January 1726, did not write about a chest either; see also chapter 7.

water on the island. The latter information Hasenbosch must have got from someone familiar with the survival of William Dampier and his men in 1701. Unfortunately, nobody could inform Hasenbosch about the location of this source of water.

When reading the diary, we see the condition of Hasenbosch slowly go down, due to a lack of fresh water. Food was but a minor problem, because he could kill turtles and birds and collect the eggs of both. He had to make long walks to find water but found very little. He probably rarely went far into the east and southeast parts of the island, because of the steep slopes over there. He discovered goats on 2 July 1725, 56 days after his marooning, in high places in the interior of the island. Almost certainly, the goats generally stayed in the high regions near the strong water spring in Breakneck Valley.

Let us have a closer look at Hasenbosch's problems:
- his housing;
- his water shortage;
- his consumption of turtles;
- his consumption of birds and eggs;
- his consumption of vegetables;
- his consumption of rice;
- his need for fuel;
- his footwear;
- his psychological problems.

Hasenbosch's housing.
On his first day, 5 May 1725, Hasenbosch set up his tent on the very south end of Long Beach, in a sort of cave in the large rock formation that separated Long Beach from Deadman's Beach. A few days later he moved his tent to Deadman's Beach, close to the other side of the rock formation. His tent seems to have stood there for the rest of Hasenbosch's stay, although he did not sleep in it every night. On or around 26 June, Hasenbosch probably moved his camp to Dampier's

Cave, in the neighbourhood of Middleton's Ridge, in the middle of the island, close to his new source of water, Dampier's Drip. On 4 July he moved his things from the cave and installed a new abode on "another part" of the island, without indicating the exact location. However, from an entry under 19 August we can conclude it was once again a cave, this time closer to the shoreline than Dampier's Cave. Possibly it was the cave or lava tunnel near South West Bay, on the slope of Command Hill. Around 20 August, Hasenbosch seems to have returned to his tent on Deadman's Beach, which seems to have remained his home until the end.

Hasenbosch's water-problem.

According to the diary, Hasenbosch ran out of his original amount of water on 10 June 1725, 36 days after his marooning. On 10 June he found a source, almost certainly the source now called Dampier's Drip, a reservoir of rainwater, enclosed in a layer of clay. On 27 June Dampier's Drip became dry. Hasenbosch made many desperate searches for water, which were rarely successful. Unfortunately, he never found the strong water spring in Breakneck Valley, not far from the island's top. In the diary, accounts of drinking his own urine - a desperate action under such circumstances - start on 21 August. Hasenbosch had probably started suffering terribly from thirst and dehydration many weeks earlier. In the entries of the last weeks, we read about him drinking the blood of turtles and birds, to get fluids.

Hasenbosch's consumption of turtles.

In *An Authentick Relation* we read about the killing of turtles and the consumption of their meat and eggs, in the month of May, as well as in the months of August and September. However, the turtle season usually starts in December and ends in June and occasionally continues until July. There are roughly three possibilities to explain the mentioning of turtles in August and September 1725 in *An Authentick Relation*:

- Hasenbosch was confused about the dates;
- the English translator or rewriter made mistakes. The translator might also have deliberately added dates or might have imagined some turtles, to make the text more interesting;
- in 1725 there were different (or more) migration periods. Perhaps there were so many more turtles than now that there was a steady

stream throughout the year. Even today, turtles are occasionally seen – in small numbers - outside the "normal" season[48]. Of course, we will need more 18th century reports of sightings of turtles on the beaches of Ascension to get a better insight in the numbers of turtles throughout the year.

Hasenbosch's consumption of birds and bird's eggs.

As Ascension was a paradise for seabirds, collecting seabirds and eggs was one of Hasenbosch's minor problems. He probably only killed boobies, large birds that are easy to approach and kill[49]. He did not write how he killed the boobies but he probably beat them with a piece of wood or stone. He also salted many dead boobies, with salt he found along the beaches and between the rocks on the shore. The salt was brilliantly white and of excellent quality[50]. Of course, Hasenbosch ate the eggs of various bird species.

Hasenbosch's consumption of vegetables.

The survival kit of Hasenbosch included onions, peas and chickpeas and he tried to use this vegetables to start a garden. On 10 May 1725 he planted some in the ground somewhere on the south side of the island and two days later he did the same very close to his tent on Deadman's Beach. Almost certainly, these efforts failed, because we read only one time again about the gardening; under the date of 6 August we read that vermin had eaten all peas and chickpeas in the ground near his tent. It is possible that Hasenbosch ate some of his original rations of onions, peas and chickpeas but the diary does not inform us. The diary gives very little information about food other than meat or eggs. On 10 May Hasenbosch found and ate some purslane, which must have been the indigenous sort of purslane of the island (*Portulaca oleracea*)[51]. On 10 and 11 May he also saw other plants but he considered them not safe to eat.

---

[48] Information from Stedson Stroud.

[49] See chapter 2 for details about seabird species.

[50] Koolbergen, *Ibid*, p.139 and S. De Rennefort *Mémoires pour servir à des Indes Orientales*, 1688, part 1, p.242. The Frenchman Souchu de Rennefort travelled as secretary for the Council of the French East India Company and made a brief visit to Ascension and reported about the excellent salt that could be gathered at Ascension.

[51] The purslane is mentioned by early travellers to Ascension, such as Captain James Cook in 1775; see Tony Cross, *St Helena, Including Ascension Island and Tristan da Cunha*, p.146-147.

Hasenbosch's consumption of rice.

The survival kit included an unknown quantity of rice. Unlike the onions, peas and chickpeas, Hasenbosch could use the rice for direct consumption only. The consumption of boiled rice is mentioned in several entries of the diary. Perhaps Hasenbosch was careful not to boil too much rice (and eggs), because he needed his precious and scarce water for the boiling.

Hasenbosch's need for fuel.

Hasenbosch needed fuel to boil eggs, tea and rice. In *An Authentick Relation* we read entries about searches for firewood under the dates of 13 June, 29 June, 10 July and 4 August; all those entries suggest that firewood was difficult to find. Under the date of 7 October we read that all wood was gone, forcing the castaway to eat raw meat and salted fowls.

Hasenbosch's footwear.

As Hasenbosch had to make long walks, his footwear must have caused many problems. It is not unlikely that he possessed more than one pair of shoes and walking barefoot is not recommended on the lava fields and rocks of Ascension. The only remark in *An Authentick Relation* about shoes is under the date of 12 June: "My shoes being worn out, the Rocks cut my feet to pieces; (…)". Under the date of 22 June we read about a long trip, during which "the Rocks [were] so sharp to my bare Feet", indicating Hasenbosch had been walking barefooted over the rocks. Unfortunately, the diary does not give us any further information about the condition of Hasenbosch's feet or shoes.

Hasenbosch's psychological problems.

Several times the diary tells about a guilty conscience and evil spirits tormenting the castaway. It is not certain that Hasenbosch wrote these passages himself. Many of those passages have a remarkably different

---

According to the Ashmoles, in their standard work standard work *St Helena and Ascension island: a natural history* purslane on Ascension was first mentioned in 1754. In those days the plant was probably more abundant than now, although the goats ate it. In the early 19th century members of the garrison used it as a salad (Ashmoles, *Ibid*, p.443).

literary style than the rest of the text. It is possible that the English translator invented most of – or even all - those passages to make the book more attractive[52].

When reading the diary, one thing is clear: with so many turtles and birds, Hasenbosch could have survived for many extra months but his health weakened very quickly due to a lack of fresh water. Moreover, he had bad luck that no ships called at Ascension during his stay.

The final entry in *An Authentick Relation* is dated 16 October 1725. Hasenbosch probably died about that date. I estimate the chance that he was rescued at less than one percent. I will discuss this possibility in chapter 8. But let us first, in chapter 7, have a close look at the discovery of the diary by British sailors in January 1726. With the information from the logs of the British ships, we are almost forced to conclude that Hasenbosch did not survive the hell of Ascension.

---

[52] In chapter 9 I will discuss the reliability of the translation of the diary in detail.

Green turtles on Ascension on a 19th century engraving. In the upper picture we see the animals (all females) coming on land. In the bottom left we see the large-scale butchering. In the bottom right we see a "turned" turtle (from Koolbergen's book).

CHAPTER 7. January 1726: British mariners discover the diary on Ascension

According to many writings between the 1730s and now, the skeleton and the diary of the "unknown Dutch castaway on Ascension in 1725" were found by crew members of the English ship *Compton*, commanded by Captain Mawson, in January 1726. For example, the story of the skeleton was included in Charles Neider, *Great Shipwrecks and Castaways* (1951), in Lawrence G. Green, *South African Beachcomber* (1958), in Lawrence G. Green, *Islands Time Forgot* (1962), in Bernard Stonehouse, *Wideawake Island; The Story of the B.O.U. Centenary Expedition to Ascension* (1960), in Duff Hart-Davis, *Ascension, the story of a South Atlantic island* (1972) and in Edward E. Leslie, *Desperate Journeys, Abandoned Souls* (1988). Somewhere in the 1990s Michiel Koolbergen decided to do something that earlier authors referring to the Dutch castaway had never done: examine the log of the *Compton* in the India Office Library and Record in London! By doing so, Koolbergen found out that the *Compton* and her captain were genuine. He also found some other interesting and surprising information.

In early January 1726 the English East India ship *Compton* was sailing in the South Atlantic Ocean, bound for England. The ship left the island of Saint Helena, a resupply station of the English East India Company, on 11 January 1726[53]. Captain William Mawson and his crew had a serious problem; the *Compton* was severely leaking, in spite of repairs carried out by workers on Saint Helena. Fortunately, the *Compton* remained within view of another English East India ship, the *James and Mary*, commanded by Captain John Balchen[54]. The two captains decided to keep their ships together and on 15 January Captain Mawson of the *Compton* was even temporarily on board the *James and Mary*. Doubtless, the two captains

---

[53] All dates in this chapter are in the *Julian* (old) calendar, which was still used in Britain at that time. The Julian calendar was 11 days behind the modern calendar. Strictly speaking, it was still 1725 for the British, because they started a new year on 25 March. However, I have used "1726" throughout the entire text, although it was still 1725 in the British calendar.

[54] In fact, Balchen had been one of Mawson's highest-ranking officers some months before but became captain of the *James and Mary* when her Captain Thomas Aubone died at sea on 19 August 1725 (Julian date, 11 days behind the modern calendar).

thought of the possibility that all people on board the *Compton* might have to move to the *James and Mary*. On the night of 15 January, the two ships changed course for Ascension Island, where the *Compton* had to be made seaworthy again. On the afternoon of 19 January, the two ships anchored in Clarence Bay, the common anchoring spot. Both captains sent men ashore to "turn turtles". And then, the men on shore made an astonishing discovery, described by Captain Mawson[55] in the log of the *Compton*, dated 20 January:

> We found a Tent a Shore in the Bay and Bed[d]ing in it [,] a Tea Kettle and Tea. Pipes [,] a Hatchet and Nails and several other things, with some Writeing [sic] Papers by which we found the Dutch Fleet the fifth of May last their stile [the Dutch calendar – A.R.] had put a Shore one of their Men for some Crime he had Committed on board. His Writing continue to November but we have no Dutch enough amongst us to read them. We made search in several places to find the Man or his Body but could not and we doe beleive [sic] he is not gon off the Island because his Paper and a great many Necessary are left in the Tent.

On the same date (20 January 1726) Captain Balchen wrote in the log of the *James and Mary*:

> (…) here we found a Tent with Bedding and Several Books – with some Writings by which we find there was a Dutch Man turn[ed] on Shore here out of a Dutch Ship, for being guilty of Sodomy in last May. Could not find him so beleive [sic] he Perished for want of water.

The logs mention a diary, a tent and various belongings *but no man or skeleton*! As the logs were official documents that had to be given to the East India Company after arrival in England, there is no reason to doubt the truth of the logs. When we combine the - doubtless reliable - information of the logs of the *Compton* and the *James and Mary*, we can conclude that the English found a "camp" of an unknown Dutchman, left behind by a Dutch ship, as a punishment for some crime. According to the log of the *James and Mary* the crime of the unknown Dutchman

---

[55] Interestingly, the log of the *Compton* also mentioned, under the date 20 January 1725, that the cross at "the hill" (doubtless Cross Hill) had been taken down.

84

was *sodomy*; obviously, some crewmember with knowledge of Dutch read parts of the diary and drew the conclusion that the unknown Dutchman had been punished for sodomy. According to the log of the *Compton*, the diary started on 5 May 1725 (Dutch calendar) and ended in November 1725; the English version of the diary of 1728, published as *An Authentick Relation* starts on 5 May 1725 and ends on 14 October 1725.

The British mariners repaired the *Compton*. Not surprisingly, men of both ships also made use of the opportunity to "turn turtles", to have fresh meat for some time; each ship got five living turtles on board. The men also searched for the mysterious Dutch castaway or his remains but found nothing.

On 22 January 1726 the *Compton* and the *James and Mary* sailed away from Ascension, bound for England. The *Compton* and the *James and Mary* reached Woolwich (London) on 9 April 1726 and 23 April 1726, respectively. The diary was on board one of the ships and would soon start a life of its own.

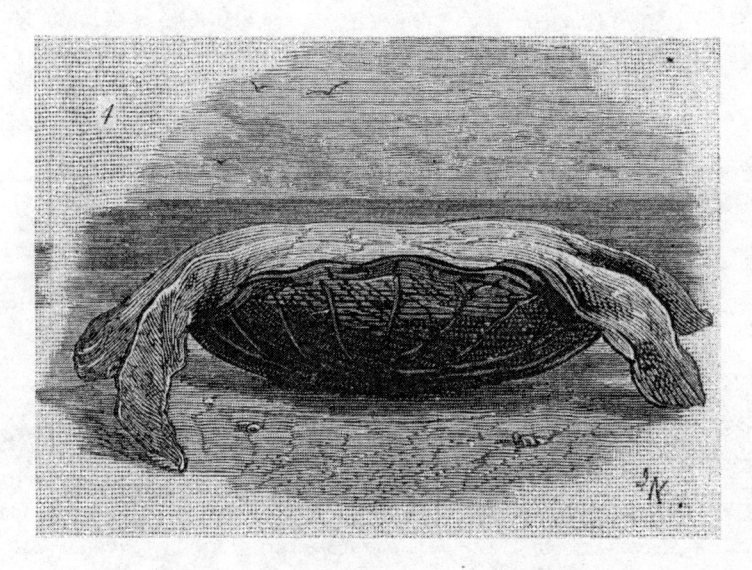

A "turned" turtle on a 19th century picture. The animals – all females on land for nesting - were turned around, brought on board and could be kept alive for up to six weeks until the cook slaughtered them (from Koolbergen's book).

> **Thursday the 20th** — At Day light Pumped out the Ship and put her on the Careen and put Passling under the Cant under the Wale and filled up the Sheathing and Caulked it and Paid it and under the Ships Counter on the Larboard Side under Water found the Sheathing open and the Seam for about eighteen Inches, so open as at one blow struck the Chisell up to the Head which is a place where the Ship certainly made a great deal of Water turned ten Tortoises which were devided between the James and Mary and our selves. We found a Tent a Shore in the Bay and Beding in it a Tea Kettle and Tea, Pipes, a Hatchet and Nails and several other things with some Writeing Papers by which we found the Dutch Fleet the fifth of May last their Stile had put a Shore one of their Men for some Crime he had committed on board, his Writing continue to November but we have not Dutch enough amongst us to read them. we made search in several places to find the Man or his Body but could not and we doe beleve he is not gon off the Island because his Paper and a great many Necessary are left in the Tent. in the Evening Wrighted Ship and found she had made no Water.

> Fair weather the winds between the SE & E. At 3 Yesterday in the Afternoon anchord on the NW Side of the Island Ascention. Dist: off Shore one Mile Depth of water 30 fathom, fine black oz Ground, here is a fine Sandy bay and good Landing with Your boats, Sent our Boat on Shore to Turn Turtle; this Morning the Boat Returnd onboard with two Left Eight on Shore which we fetched off afterwards, here we found a Tent with Bedding and Several Books with Some Writings by which we find there was a Dutch Man turnd on Shore here out of a Dutch Ship for being guilty of Sodomy in Last May. Could not find him so believe he Perished for want of water; the Compton is now on the heel a Stoping her Leak, this Evening Sent People on Shore to turn Turtle,

The upper picture shows part of the log of the English East India vessel "Compton", written by Captain William Mawson. The lower picture shows part of the log of the English East India vessel "James and Mary", written by Captain John Balchen. In both logs we read about the discovery of the diary on 20 January 1725/26 (English calendar, in the modern calendar it was eleven days later). (From Koolbergen's book, Koolbergen draw this from the India Office Library and Records in London, catalogue numbers L/MAR/B/666A and L/MAR/B/676B).

CHAPTER 8. When, where and how did Leendert Hasenbosch die?

Personally, I am more than 99 percent sure that at the end of 1725 Leendert Hasenbosch either committed suicide or died due to thirst or dehydration. For many years we thought to have *proof* of the castaway's death, because the legend told that his skeleton was found next to his diary. However, the logs of the *Compton* and the *James and Mary* clearly state that no skeleton was found, in spite of searches. Perhaps the skeleton was simply too far from the landing spot. Besides, the skeleton might have become unrecognisable by the time the British mariners were searching or it might have been washed away by the sea.

There is a passage in a book, written by a Swedish priest and naturalist, Per Osbeck, which might refer to Leendert Hasenbosch. Osbeck visited the island in 1752 and his narrative was published later. In his book, Osbeck described the same rocky structure with caves that was close to the tent of Hasenbosch in 1725, near the usual landing spot at Clarence Bay, between Long Beach and Deadman's Beach. Duff Hart-Davis, in *Ascension, The story of a South Atlantic island* (1972), wrote that one legend written by Osbeck might have been a distorted echo of the story of the Dutch castaway. Hart-Davis wrote in his book:

> In that [cave] which was next the shore were several French and English letters, of last year, as advices to new-comers: the upper one [cave] is said to have been the habitation of an English supercargo, who some years ago was left there as a punishment for a detestable crime [the German edition of Osbeck's book wrote "sodomy" – A.R.[56]], with some victuals and an ax, to kill tortoises, which he was forced to roast by the heat of the sun on the mountains. It is likewise related that another nation afterwards helped him away.

Roughly speaking, there are four possible explanations for Osbeck's story:

---

[56] Osbeck, *Reise nach Ostindien und China*, 1765, p.376.

- the story of the English supercargo is pure fiction;
- the story of the English supercargo is true. This is not impossible, because the English authorities, as the Dutch ones, did not want sodomy on their ships;
- the story refers to Leendert Hasenbosch. In that case the story must have been passed on a number of times, transforming a "Dutch bookkeeper" into an "English supercargo";
- a combination of the latter two explanations.

Personally, I estimate the chances for the last two explanations to be quite low. In short, I think that Hasenbosch died in late 1725, because:

- although the text and the dates of *An Authenthick Relation* can not be trusted 100 percent, I think *An Authentick Relation* is reliable enough to presume that the life of Hasenbosch was in peril, due to thirst and dehydration;
- the story of the Swedish priest Per Osbeck about the English supercargo is quite remarkable and interesting but I do not think the story has anything to do with Hasenbosch. For example, according to *An Authentick Relation* Hasenbosch stayed in the grotto inside the rock formation between Long Beach from Deadman's Beach for only a few days in early May 1725, whereas the English supercargo would have stayed much longer in the same grotto;
- if Hasenbosch was rescued, it is difficult to imagine why he left so many things – probably *all* his possessions – behind on Deadman's Beach. For example, in the log of the *Compton* we read that many "necessities" were still in the tent. In the log of the *James and Mary* we read that there were still books in the tent; those books were almost certainly one or more bibles and prayer books and it is difficult to understand why Hasenbosch would have left them behind. We must also keep in mind, that if Hasenbosch was rescued, his rescuers almost certainly landed at the usual landing spot, from where his rescuers must have seen the tent and the other things of Hasenbosch. One can imagine the faces of his rescuers seeing the castaway coming on board without many useful possessions!

- if Hasenbosch was rescued, it is difficult to imagine why the story of his rescue was never published. The rescue of a castaway was a rare and spectacular happening, often leading to publications. For example, the life and rescue of the Scotchman Alexander Selkirk, after a solitary life for almost five years (1704-1709) on Juan Fernandez Island, were published in 1718 in Woodes Rogers's book *A Cruising Voyage Round the World*, making Selkirk's story famous[57]. If Hasenbosch had been picked up by some ship, we must conclude that the ship went down with all hands before she reached a port![58]

We could be 100 percent sure of the death of Hasenbosch on Ascension (or in its surrounding sea), if we knew for certain that no ship called at Ascension between 5 May 1725 and 30 January 1726. This would mean looking in archives in countries that might have had ships near Ascension, like Portugal, France and Sweden.

I hope that one day groups of researchers will start reading *all* – British, Dutch and other - nonprinted logs of ships that passed Ascension before about 1830, because this is the only way to answer many questions about the island's early history. How often was Ascension visited? Was Ascension *really* often used as a place of exile for criminals? Is Osbeck's story of the English supercargo true? How often did mariners organise hunts of birds and goats? Were there many turtles on the beaches outside the present season? And so on.

---

[57] See chapter 13 for details.

[58] Duff Hart-Davis, in *Ascension, the story of a South Atlantic island*, p.22 wrote that he was not sure if the diary contained the truth. Among other things he wrote: "Is it altogether too sceptical to suppose that the castaway fabricated the entire journal and left it behind, when he was rescued, in the hope of eventually disconcerting the people who had marooned him?" This possibility is extremely unlikely, especially because of the evidence from the logs of the British ships. Hart-Davis's idea would be more likely if the British had *only* found a diary. However, they found many more things that must have belonged to the castaway. Hart-Davis was also sceptical because of the diary's entries about turtles in August and September, outside the season. However, in 1725 the turtles might have had no season at all; even today they are seen occasionally outside the season (see chapters 5 and 6). By the way, in my view the published diary cannot be trusted for 100 percent either. However, my prime suspicion focuses on the entries about the guilty conscience and the evil spirits; in my view, it is not very likely that Hasenbosch wrote so much about those issues himself – see chapter 9 for details.

AN
Authentick Relation
Of the many
Hardships and Sufferings
OF A
DUTCH SAILOR,

Who was put on Shore on the uninhabited Isle of *Ascension*, by Order of the Commadore of a Squadron of *Dutch* Ships.

WITH

A Remarkable ACCOUNT of his Converse with APPARITIONS and EVIL SPIRITS, during his Residence on the Island.

AND

A particular DIARY of his TRANSACTIONS from the Fifth of *May* to the Fourteenth of *October*, on which Day he perished in a miserable Condition.

Taken from the Original JOURNAL *found in his Tent by some Sailors, who landed from on Board the* Compton, *Captain* Morson *Commander, in* January 172⅘.

LONDON:

Printed for J. ROBERTS, near the *Oxford-Arms* in *Warwick-Lane*.   M.DCC.XXVIII.

(*Price Six-Pence.*)

Title page of "An Authentick Relation" published in London in 1728 by John Roberts (from Koolbergen's book).

A COPY OF A JOURNAL, &c.

Saturday, **May 5.**

BY Order of the Commadore and Captains of the *Dutch* Fleet, I was set on Shore on the Island of *Ascension*, which gave me a great deal of Dissatisfaction, but I hope Almighty God will be my Protection. They put ashore with me a Cask of Water, two Buckets, and an old Frying-Pan, &c. I made my Tent on the Beach near a Rock, wherein I put some of my Clothes.

The first date of the diary – Saturday, 5 May 1725 – of the Dutch castaway, as it was published – under the title "An Authentick Relation" - in London in 1728 by John Roberts (from Koolbergen's book).

CHAPTER 9. 1726-1728: Did Daniel Defoe fictionalise the Dutch diary?

In April 1726 the English East Indiamen *Compton* and the *James and Mary* reached Woolwich (London). One of the two ships had the diary of the unknown Dutch castaway on Ascension Island on board. About two years later, somewhere during the year 1728, books of the hardships of a lonely Dutch sailor left behind on Ascension Island in 1725, entitled *An Authentick Relation* were published in London and Dublin.

No doubt, *An Authentick Relation* is a translation or an adaptation of the Dutch diary of Leendert Hasenbosch. Unfortunately, we do not know what happened with the original diary between 1726 and 1728. However, Michiel Koolbergen had a hypothesis about that and I strongly support that hypothesis. In fact, the title of this chapter already reveals that hypothesis. The complete title of *An Authentick Relation* reads:

> *An Authentick Relation of the many Hardships and Sufferings of a Dutch Sailor, Who was put on Shore on the uninhabited Isle of Ascension, by Order of the Commadore of a Squadron of Dutch Ships. – with – A Remarkable Account of his Converse with Apparitions and Evil Spirits, during his Residence on the Island. - and – A particular Diary of his Transactions from the Fifth of May to the Fourteenth of October, on which Day he perished in a miserable Condition. – Taken from the Original Journal found in his Tent by some Sailors, who landed from on Board the Compton, Captain Morson Commander, in January 1725/6.*

On the title page of the London edition we can also read the publisher (J. Roberts, "near the Oxford-Arms in Warwick-Lane"), as well as the year of edition (MDCCXXVIII or 1728) and the price (Six-Pence). The London edition has 28 pages.

To modern standards, the complete title of *An Authentick Relation* is quite long but in the 18th century such long titles were very common. A long title was a marketing tool, comparable with the summary on the back cover of a modern book. A long title had to convince a potential buyer about the quality of the book. And so, contemporary authors and publishers were keen on creating attractive titles for their books. Interestingly, the title page of *An Authentick Relation* puts the death of the castaway on 14 October 1725. Perhaps that date was the last date of the original diary but that does not necessarily mean that the author died that day. The preface of *An Authentick Relation* is also quite interesting and makes us believe that we have to do with a perfect translation of the original Dutch diary. The preface reads:

> To the Reader. As the following Journal carries all possible Marks of Truth and Sincerity in it; so we have thought fit to publish it exactly as it was wrote, by the miserable Wretch, who is the Subject of it, without adding any borrowed Descriptions of Places, Coasts, &c. which is too frequently done in Pieces of this Nature, in order to increase their bulk.
>
> The detestable Crime for which the Dutch Commodore thought fit to abandon and leave this Sailor on a desert Island, is pretty plainly pointed out, p.15 of the Journal. The Miseries and Hardships he lingered under for more than five Months, were so unusually terrible, that the bear Reading his Account of'em must make the hardest Heart melt with Compassion. Tormented with excessive Thirst; in want for almost every Thing necessary to defend him from the Inclemency of the Weather; left to the severe Upbraidings and Reflections of a guilty Conscience; harassed by the blasphemous Conversations of evil Sprits, haunted by Apparitions, even tumbled up and down in his Tent by Demons; and at the same time not one Person upon the Island from whom to seek Consolation or Advice: There are such Calamities, as no Mortal could ever long support himself under. But at the same time the fatal Catastrophe of this Man recommends to us, the preserving that Wall of Brass (as the Poet calls it) which will be a Comfort to us under all Misfortunes, viz. a Conscience free from Guilt.
>
> ---------------- **Hic Murus Aheneus esto,**
> Nil conscribe sibi, nulla pallescere culpa.
>
> N.B. The Original Manuscript, from which this Journal was printed, may be seen at the Publisher's.

At the end of the preface, we read part of a Roman poem about the comfort of having a conscience free from guilt, written by the Roman poet Quintus Horatius Flaccus (65-8 B.C.). To be exact, we read lines 60 and 61 of the first letter of the first book of *Epistulae*, a letter to the poet's do-gooder Maecenas[59].

In 1728 *An Authentick Relation* was also published in Dublin. The Dublin edition has the same title and text as the London edition but the Dublin edition only has 22 pages; 6 pages less than the London edition, due to a different layout. At the bottom of the title page of the Dublin edition we read; "The Eighth Edition / London: Printed; And Dublin Reprinted and sold by George Falkner in Christ-Church-Tard, 1728"[60]. The statement that the Dublin edition would be the *eighth* edition is almost certainly untrue. In those days such claims were sometimes placed on the title page of a book, in order to increase its marketability[61].

Is *An Authentick Relation* is a *reliable* translation or adaptation of the diary of Hasenbosch? As we do not have the original diary any more, we will never be certain. It is possible that some entries were added or "enhanced", such as the entries about apparitions of former acquaintances and the evil spirits. Firstly, those entries have a higher literary value than the entries about walking over the island, killing birds and turtles and so on. Secondly, the apparitions and evil spirits make the book more thrilling and more fun to read. And throughout the ages, thrilling books have always been better marketable than dull ones!

We will probably never know *who* was – or were - responsible for the translation or rewriting of the Dutch diary but all circumstantial evidence is pointing to the renowned master-storyteller and voluminous writer

---

[59] Koolbergen, *Ibid*, p.48

[60] Unfortunately, we do not know the *dates* of the publication of the London and Dublin editions. Presumably, publisher George Faulkner in Dublin had a "gentleman's agreement" with publisher John Roberts in London and in that case the Dublin edition came *later* than the London one. However, sometimes pirate editions of English books were published in Ireland *before* the English books and smuggled into England. So, there is a small chance that the Dublin edition of *An Authentick Relation* is an example of such a pirate edition. This possibility was not mentioned by Koolbergen, who was probably unaware of this curiosity, which was a result of the fact that the contemporary English copyright legislation was not applicable in Ireland (although Ireland had already formed a United Kingdom with England and Wales). See Constantina Maxwell, *Dublin under the Georges*, 1956 (1997 edition), p.202.

[61] Koolbergen got this information about falsehoods on title pages from a conservator of the 18th century literature of the British Library in London (Koolbergen, *Ibid*, p.256).

Daniel Defoe (c.1660-1731) *himself*. In short, we have the following circumstantial evidence:

- In 1728 Defoe was in his late sixties but still active. Being the author of the famous novel *Robinson Crusoe*, first published in 1719, he was of course an expert on marooned sailors. In fact, both *Robinson Crusoe* and *An Authentick Relation* describe the adventures of a castaway, written by himself[62];
- Defoe was familiar with the Dutch language[63] and he possessed Dutch books, including a grammar book and a dictionary;
- *An Authentick Relation* was published by John Roberts from London, who was also Defoe's principal publisher at the time;
- in the final pages of the Dublin edition of *An Authentick Relation*, forthcoming books were announced, including Defoe's book (without the name of Defoe) *The history of Moll Flanders*;
- towards the end of his life, Daniel Defoe often had books published that were partly written by others and rewritten by him. I will give details below;
- the writing style of the remarks about the guilty conscience of the author, with apparitions and evil spirits might well be "Defoenian". I will give details below;
- one section of *An Authentick Relation* has a remarkable resemblance with the famous *footprint incident* in the novel *Robinson Crusoe*. I will give details below.

Towards the end of his life, Daniel Defoe was a master in collecting strange stories and rudimentary notations and preparing them for publication by rewriting. Two important examples are the huge books *The Four Voyages of Capt. George Roberts* (1726), *Madagascar: Or, Robert Drury's Journal, during Fifteen years Captivity on That Island* (1729). According to many critics, the books by the mysterious "George Roberts" and

---

[62] It should be kept in mind that in those days Defoe's name was often not on his novels. Many contemporaries considered his fictitious narrators to be genuine, because Defoe's name was not in the book. Examples of such novels are *Robinson Crusoe*, *Captain Singleton* and *Moll Flanders*.

[63] Koolbergen, *Ibid*, p.104 and p.255 and Broos, in *Robinson Crusoe in the old and new worlds*, The Hague, 1992, pp.13-34. Defoe once visited the United Provinces as a spy.

"Robert Drury" might be partly written by real narrators, referring to real adventures. However, both books were rewritten by Defoe, who probably added some things imagined by him[64]. In his adaptations he often crossed the border between truth and fiction but he seems not to have had any guilty feelings for doing so, as James Sutherland wrote in *Daniel Defoe, A Critical Study* (1971):

> In 1724, indeed, he had become so accustomed to living in a twilight world between fact and fiction that the two mingle imperceptibly in his mind. To some extent he may have become the victim of his own narrative technique. Early in the nineteenth century a writer in *Gentleman's Magazine* defended the authenticity of *Robert Drury's Journal* by claiming that it had "all that simplicity and verbiage.... expected in narratives of the illiterate, but none of the artifices of fiction". But by 1729 Defoe was expert at imitating the simplicity and verbiage of illiterate narrators. Much earlier than that, a hostile journalist had made a sneering reference to "the little art he is true master of, of forging a story and imposing it on the world for truth".[65]

Another example of the writings of such an "illiterate narrator", rewritten by Defoe, might well have been the diary of the Dutch castaway on Ascension!

The apparitions and evil spirits in *An Authentick Relation* look very "Defoenian". Although Defoe believed in the existence of supernatural spirits and apparitions, Defoe also thought that spirits and apparitions that were confronting remorseful criminals with their crimes only existed in the minds of those criminals. In other words, Defoe thought that remorseful criminals often saw, heard or felt nonexistent spirits and apparitions. One of Defoe's books about spirits and apparitions was published in 1727 by John Roberts, under the long title *An Essay on the History and Reality of Apparitions. Being An Account of what they are and what they are not. As Also How we may distinguish between the Apparitions of Good and Evil Spirits and how we ought to behave to them. With a great Variety of Surprizing*

---

[64] James Sutherland, *Daniel Defoe, A Critical Study*, 1971, pp.152-153. Another book, *A General History of the Robberies and Murders of the Most Notorious Pyrates* (2 volumes, 1724 and 1728), written by the mysterious Captain Charles Johnson was entirely written by Defoe, as was convincingly proven in 1939, by professor John Robert Moore. Captain Charles Johnson never existed.

[65] Sutherland, *Ibid*, p.153.

and Diverting Examples, never Publish'd before. The book has some 400 pages and includes a thrilling illustration next to the title page; a drawing of the ghost of Caesar (as a victim of murder) in the tent of Brutus (Caesar's murderer)!

Let us suppose that Defoe read the diary of the unknown Dutchman in order to prepare it for publication. In that case, Defoe must soon have concluded that the Dutchman had committed sodomy[66]. And so, Defoe must have thought that the Dutchman must have been haunted by a guilty conscience, "allowing" Defoe to include some apparitions and evil spirits in both the main text and the title page. If the original diary *did* contain some entries that could be interpreted as reflections of a guilty conscience, it is possible that Defoe decided to blow those entries up to a much larger and thrilling scale.

There is a passage in *An Authentick Relation* that shows such a remarkable resemblance with the famous *footprint incident* in *Robinson Crusoe* that we have sufficient reason to think that both were written by the same person, i.e. Daniel Defoe. This crucial passage in *An Authentick Relation* reads:

> The 16th Ditto [16 June 1725 – A.R.], To no purpose looked for Ships; and in the Night was surprised by a Noise round my Tent of Cursing and Swearing and the most blasphemous Conversations that I ever heard. My Concern was so great, that I thought I should have died with the Fright. I did nothing but offer up my Prayers to the Almighty to protect me in this miserable Circumstance; but my fright rendered me in a very bad Condition of praying, I trembling to that degree, that I could not compose my Thoughts; and any body would have believed that the Devil had moved his Quarters and was coming to keep Hell on Ascension. I was certain that there was no human Creature on the Island but myself, having not seen the Footsteps of any Man but my own; and so much libidinous Talk was impossible to be expressed by any body but Devils. And to my greater Surprise I was certain that I

---

[66] See also Chapter 7. In the log of the *James and Mary* it is stated the Dutchman had been left behind on the island for sodomy, so we may conclude that the original diary probably *did* contain reference to the castaway's act(s) of sodomy. However, I doubt whether the castaway was tormented with his guilty conscience as much as some parts of *An Authentick Relation* let us believe. It seems that the British publisher liked to publish about the subject of a guilty conscience – see, for example, also the preface of the booklet.

was very well acquainted with one of the Voiced, it bearing a affinity of an intimate Acquaintance of mine; and I really thought that I was sometimes touched by an invisible Spirit. I made my application to the Father, Son and Holy Ghost for forgiveness of my Sins and that they would protect me from these evil Spirits. It was three a Clock in the Morning before they ceased tormenting me and then being very weary, I fell to sleep. In the Morning I awoke about seven a-clock and returned God Almighty my hearty and sincere Thanks for his last Night's Protection of me, but still heard some Shrieks near my Tent, but could see nothing. I took my Prayer Book and read the Prayers proper for a Man in my Condition and at the same time heard a Voice, crying, Bouger. I can't afford paper enough to set down every particular of this unhappy Day.

As the text above, the famous *footprint incident* in *Robinson Crusoe* tells about fear for the Devil. In that incident, the 42-year old Robinson Crusoe, knowing to have been alone on his island for already 15 years, suddenly saw a footprint that is not his! The psychological impact on Robinson Crusoe is enormous. The passage itself reads[67]:

It happened one day, about noon, going towards my boat, I was exceedingly surprised with the print of a man's naked foot on the shore, which was very plain to be seen in the sand. I stood like one thunderstruck, or as I had seen an apparition: I listened, I looked round me, but I could hear nothing, nor see anything; I went up to a rising ground, to look farther; I went up to the shore and down the shore, but it was all one; I could see no other impression than that one. I went to it again to see of there were any more, and to observe if it might not be my fancy; but there was no room for that, for there was exactly the print of a foot, toes, heel, and every part of a foot: how it came thither, I knew not, nor could I in the least imagine; but, after innumerable fluttering thoughts, like a man perfectly confused and out of myself, I came home to my fortification, not feeling, as we say, the ground I went on, but terrified to the last degree; looking behind me at every two or three steps, mistaking every bush and tree, and fancying every stump at a distance to be a man. Nor is it possible to describe how many various shapes my affrighted imagination represented things to me in,

---

[67] The text is in modern American English, because I drew it from the *Robinson Crusoe* edition of Doubleday and Company, inc., Garden City, New York, 1946, illustrated by Fritz Kreidel, pp.107-108.

how many wild ideas were found every moment in my fancy, and what strange unaccountable whimsies came into my thoughts by the way.

When I came to my castle (for so I think I called it after this), I fled into it like one pursued; whether I went over by the ladder, as first contrived, or went in at the hole in the rock, which I had called a door, I cannot remember; no, nor could I remember the next morning; for never frightened hare fled to cover, or fox to earth with more terror of mind than I to this retreat.

I slept none that night: the farther I was from the occasion of my fright, the greater my apprehensions were; which is something contrary to the nature of such things, and especially to the usual practice of all the thing, that I formed nothing but dismal imaginations to myself, even though I was now a great way off it. Sometimes I fancied it must be the devil, and reason joined in with me upon this supposition; for how could any other thing in human shape come into the place? Where was the ship that brought them? What marks were there of any other footsteps? And how was it possible that a man should come there? But then to think that Satan should take human shape upon him in such a place, where there could be no manner of occasion for it, but to leave the print of the foot behind him, and that even for no purpose too, for he could not be sure I would see it, - this was an amusement the other way. I considered that the Devil might have found abundance of other ways to have terrified me than this of the single print of a foot; that as I lived quite on the other side of the island, he would never have been so simple as to leave a mark in a place where it was ten thousand to one whether I should ever see it or not, and in the sand too, which the first surge of the sea, upon a high wind, would have defaced entirely: all this seemed inconsistent with the thing itself, and with all the notions we usually entertain of the subtlety of the Devil.

Abundance of such things as these assisted to argue me out of all apprehensions of its being the Devil; and I presently concluded, then, that it must be some more dangerous creature, viz. that it must be some of the savages of the main land over against me, who had wandered out to sea in their canoes, and either driven by the currents or by contrary winds, had made the island, and had been on shore, but were gone away again to sea; being as loath, perhaps, to have stayed in this desolate island as I would have been to have had them.

The passage in *An Authentick Relation* seems a smart variation of the *footprint incident* in *Robinson Crusoe*, in particular because of the sentence "I was certain that there was no human Creature on the Island but myself, having not seen the Footsteps of any Man but my own; and so much libidinous Talk was impossible to be expressed by any body but Devils". In the *footprint incident*, the narrator thinks for a short time that the footprint must have been made by the Devil himself and in *An Authentick Relation* the narrator thinks for a short time that the "libidinous Talk" could only have been produced by the Devil himself. Moreover, in this passage in *An Authentick Relation* we also read about "Footsteps of any Man but my own"; the phenomenon of an unidentified footstep is inextricably linked to the fear for the Devil.

In my view, it is very unlikely that Leendert Hasenbosch ever wrote such a "Defoenian" entry with devils and footsteps! I think that some English writer has rewritten the castaway's diary. I also think the most likely rewriter is Defoe. Hopefully, one day we will hear the astonishing news of the re-discovery of the original diary of Leendert Hasenbosch. My guess is that we will conclude that he hardly – or never - wrote about a guilty conscience or evil spirits!

If *An Authentick Relation* is a fictionalised version of the original diary, then it was child's play compared to the legends published in later years.

Many illustrated editions of Robinson Crusoe *contain illustrations of the "footprint incident". Here is one of the many examples (from Koolbergen's book).*

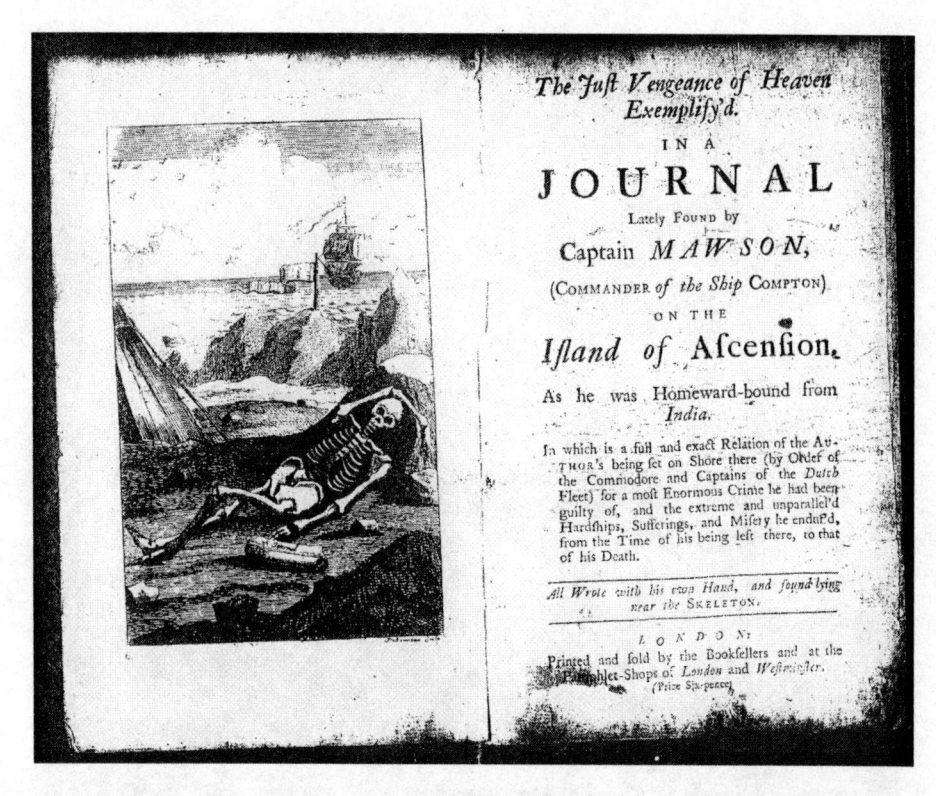

The 1730 version of the diary, published in London under the title "The Just Vengeance of Heaven Exemplify'd". It is a fake version, with many devils added by the unknown rewriter. In fact, it is a horror-story and an autobiography of a remorseful criminal tormented by devils and demons. The title page and illustration suggest that captain Mawson and his crew found a skeleton; in reality they only found a tent with the castaway's things, including the diary (from Koolbergen's book).

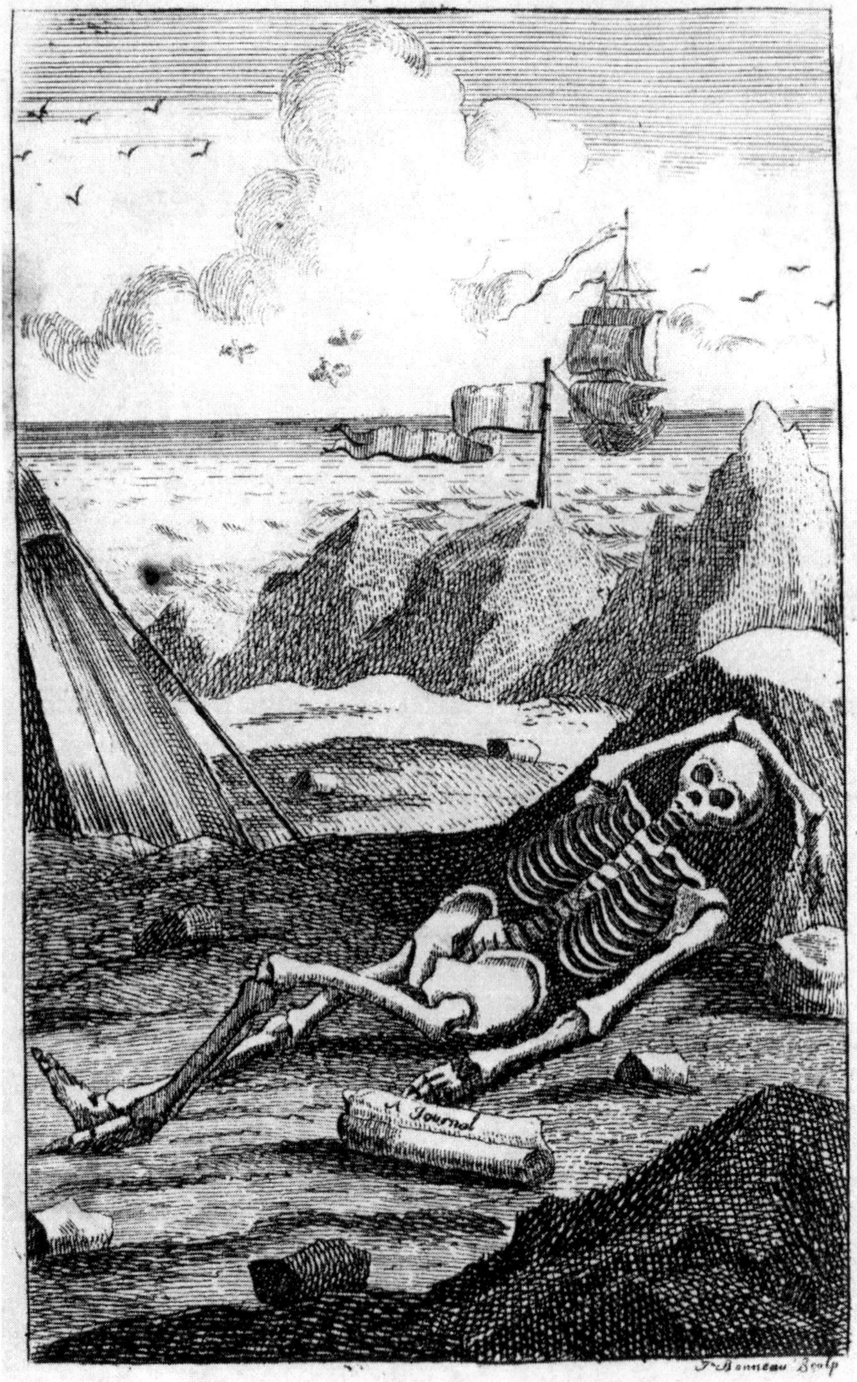
A Journal

CHAPTER 10. 1730 and 1978: the story of the Dutch castaway is faked

In 1730, about two years after the publication of *An Authentic Relation*, a new version of the history of the Dutch castaway on Ascension was published in London, entitled The *Just Vengeance of Heaven Exemplify'd*. In the new book the unfortunate castaway is haunted by many more "apparitions" and "evil spirits" than in *An Authentick Relation*. In fact, the new book was a real horror story. The complete title of the new version was:

> *The Just Vengeance of Heaven Exemplify'd. In a Journal Lately Found by Captain Mawson (Commander of the Ship Compton), on the Island of Ascension, As he was Homeward-bound from India. In which is a full and exact relation of the Author's being set on Shore there (by Order of the Commodore and Captains of the Dutch Fleet), for a most Enormous Crime he had been guilty of and the extreme and unparallel'd Hardships, Sufferings and Misery he endur'd from the Time of his being left there, to that of his Death. All Wrote with his own Hand and found lying near the Skeleton.*

At he bottom of the title page we further read:

> London; Printed and sold by the Booksellers and at the Pamphlet-Shops of London and Westminster. (Price Six-pence).

The last sentence of the title says that the diary was found "lying near the Skeleton", which is a pertinent lie and a perfect example of history falsification; in reality, Captain Mawson never found a man or skeleton! Many later authors would persistently repeat the myth of the skeleton lying next to the diary. Next to the title page of *The Just Vengeance of Heaven Exemplify'd* we even see a beautiful picture of a skeleton pointing with one of its fingers to an enrolled "Journal", with a ship in full sail in the background, arriving too late for a rescue; a beautiful and horrifying picture but far from reality!

The foreword of *The Just Vengeance of Heaven Exemplify'd* is completely different from the foreword of *An Authentick Relation*. The complete foreword of *The Just Vengeance of Heaven Exemplify'd* reads:

> As it is necessary for every one who publishes a Book to make an Apology for what he thinks erroneous, the Publisher begs leave to inform the Reader, that the Person who is the supposed Author of this Journal, by whose Skeleton it was found, was a Sailor and a Man of a very mean Capacity, as will appear, both by the false Orthography and Grammar, to any one who has Curiosity enough to see the Original. The publisher has made as little Variation as possible, because he would not in the least deviate from the Original. It may be objected by some who delight in Rhetorical Expressions, that it is penn'd in too low a Stile; but that Objection will certainly be wav'd by every one who gives himself time to consider, that Sailors for the most part are far from being Orators.
>
> It may perhaps by some be deemed fabulous on account of the frequent Apparitions mentioned to have been seen by the Author; but a Person of a small Share of reason will readily account for that, by supposing those Visions to be the effect of Distemper'd Brain, occasioned by the violent Torture both of his Mind and Body.
>
> The Copy was left in the Hands of two unhappy Gentlemen confined for Debt and is now published for their sole Benefit, whoever therefore become Purchasers of this Piece, will not only afford a comfortable Relief to them during their Confinement, but perhaps contribute to their Enlargement.

During the 1990s Michiel Koolbergen compared the printed texts of *The Just Vengeance of Heaven Exemplify'd* with the older text of *An Authentick Relation*. Koolbergen soon found out that the younger text is a very unreliable new version of the older one. As far as I know, Koolbergen's book of 2002 was the first publication mentioning the difference between the two versions. *The Just Vengeance of Heaven Exemplify'd* is more fun to read than *An Authentick Relation* but the latter is doubtless standing closer to the original Dutch text!

Here are a few examples of the numerous differences between the two versions of the diary. The text of *An Authentick Relation* under the date of 18 June reads:

> The 18th Ditto, After my Devotions went to look out and carried my Hatchet with me. On the Strand, the other Side of the Island, I found a Tree, which I believe Providence had cast ashore for me. I cut it in two Pieces, the whole being to big for me to carry. I put one half on my Shoulders and when I was half way home, set it down and rested my self on it. During which time, the Apparition appeared to me again; his Name I am afraid to utter, fearing the Event.(...)

The English writer of *The Just Vengeance of Heaven Exemplify'd* not only changed the text but also included a long and horrifying addition:

> On the 18th, after my Devotions, I went to look out as usual and took my Hatchet with me, but finding myself disappointed, made all possible Haste to the other part of the island, where to my great satisfaction I found a Tree, which I believe Providence had thrown on shore in some measures to alleviate my present Misery: I divided it with my Hatchet, the whole being more than I was capable of carrying at once: I took part of it on my Shoulder and having carried it half way to my Tent, laid it down and rested myself thereon. [addition] Alas! How wretched is that Man whose Bestial Pleasures have render'd him odious to the rest of his Fellow-Creatures and turned him loose on a barren island, Nebuchadnezzar like, to herd and graze with Beasts[68], till loathsome to himself and spurn'd by Man, he and his mis[s]pent Life calls aloud for Vengeance from on high! Such was the Case of me unhappy Wretch, which proves the Justice of All-gracious Heaven; and whilst I was resting my wearied limbs and seriously reflecting with myself, [end of addition] the Apparition appeared again to me, which gave me Horror inexpressible; his Name I am unwilling to mention, not knowing what the Consequence may be, (...)

Under the date of 20 June, we read, in both versions, about the act of sodomy of the castaway. The text of *An Authentick Relation* reads:

> (...) making use of my Fellow-Creature to satisfy my Lust, whom the Almighty Creator had ordain'd another Sex for.

---

[68] The English writer used Daniel 4:33, which in the *King James Bible* reads: "The same hour was the thing fulfilled upon Nebuchadnezzar: and he was driven from men, and did eat grass as oxen, and his body was wet with the dew of heaven, till his hairs were grown like eagles' feathers, and his nails like birds' claws."

The corresponding text of *The Just Vengeance of Heaven Exemplify'd* is different:

> (...) making use of Man to satisfy my hellish and ungovernable Lust; despising Woman, which his Hand had made a far more worthy Object.

Under the date of 30 June (1725), *An Authentick Relation* reads:

> June, the 30th, Here has been so much dry weather, to my Sorrow, that both at the Cave and the other place, where there used to be Water enough, there is now not one Drop and I am as much in want of it, as I have been since my coming to this miserable Island.

The English writer of *The Just Vengeance of Heaven Exemplify'd* probably thought the old text too dull and decided to include the apparition of a skeleton:

> On the 30th I went in Search of Water, but could find none and now all Hopes were lost, a ghastly Skeleton appear'd to me with his Hand uplifted, pointed to his Throat, an seem'd to tell me I should die with Drought.

For some reason, the English writer of *The Just Vengeance of Heaven Exemplify'd* decided to finish the diary on 14 September 1725 instead of 14 October 1725, as it had been in *An Authentick Relation*. The last words in *The Just Vengeance of Heaven Exemplify'd* were entirely invented by the English writer and read:

> (...) I cannot write much longer: I sincerely repent of the sins I committed and pray, henceforth, no Man may ever merit the Misery which I have undergone. For the Sake of which, leaving this Narrative behind me to deter Mankind from following Diabolical Inventions. I now resign my Soul to him that gave it, hoping for Mercy in - / FINIS

The diary ends abruptly, in the middle of a sentence, as if the Dutch castaway dropped his pen when he took his final breath!

After the publication of *The Just Vengeance of Heaven Exemplify'd* in 1730, there were two other publications about the Dutch castaway, both still in the 18th century. In 1746 the text of *An Authentick Relation* was included in the so-called *Harleian Miscalleny*, a London collection of rare stories. In 1748 *The Just Vengeance of Heaven Exemplify'd* was republished in Philadelphia[69].

Regrettably, most authors of later days referring to the Dutch castaway knew only one of the publications of the 18th century. The following authors of the 20th century got their information from one or both editions of *The Just Vengeance of Heaven Exemplify'd*: Charles Neider in *Great Shipwrecks and Castaways* (1951), Lawrence G. Green in both *South African Beachcomber* (1958) and *Islands Time Forgot* (1962)[70], Bernard Stonehouse in *Wideawake Island; The Story of the B.O.U. Centenary Expedition to Ascension* (1960) and Edward E. Leslie in *Desperate Journeys, Abandoned Souls* (1988). In doing so, these authors repeated the myth of the skeleton lying next to the diary, as well as the stories about the author's guilty conscience and the stories about the evil spirits, all exaggerated and far from the truth. Duff Hart-Davis, in *Ascension, the story of a South Atlantic island* (1972), got his information from the *Harleian Miscalleny* but he mentioned the discovery of the remains of the castaway[71]. Walter de la Mare, in *Desert Islands* (1930), wrote a summary of *An Authentick Relation* and hence he did not write about the discovery of a skeleton.

In 1978 Peter Agnos – pseudonym for the American author Cy A. Adler[72] - published the book *The Queer Dutchman; True Account of a Sailor castaway on a Desert Island for "Unnatural Acts" and Left to God's Mercy*, with the second title "The Queer Dutchman Castaway On Ascension". The

---

[69] On the title page we read: "London printed; Philadelphia reprinted & sold by William Badford, 1748."

[70] The South-African author Lawrence G. Green wrote in *Islands Time Forgot* about the discovery of the skeleton beside the diary by Captain Mawson of the British ship *Compton*. Green wrote: "This was another Ascension relic which I studied in the British Museum Library". When reading Green's quotations from the diary, it is clear that he did not read the original hand-written diary but a copy of *The Just Vengeance of Heaven Exemplify'd*. See Green, *Islands Time Forgot*, 1962, pp.130-132 and Green, *South African Beachcomber*, 1958, pp.181-182 and Koolbergen, *Ibid*, p.262.

[71] Hart-Davis, *Ibid*, p.18.

[72] Adler's website is www.greeneagle.org

book was reprinted in 1993. A considerable part of the text of *The Queer Dutchman* is an adaptation of *The Just Vengeance of Heaven Exemplify'd* but Peter Agnos included extra text and personalities created by himself, such as the main character Jan Svilt, his partner in his act of sodomy, his captain and his ship. The attractive preface, dated May 1977, reads:

> Four winters ago, while browsing in Mendoza's Bookstore on Anne Street in Lower Manhattan, I chanced upon a curious old book written in Dutch. The illustrations of old sailing ships, of shipwrecks and of men of cargo floundering in the sea caught my eye and I bought the book. My friend Michael Jelstra, who was born and raised in Delft, told me that the old volume was a copy of sea adventures published in Amsterdam in 1762. One story in particular intrigued me that of Jan Svilt, who was forcibly marooned on Ascension Island in 1725. Michael translated the original journal into English for me. I have added various explanatory notes and comments which I trust will add to the reader's understanding and appreciation of the journal[73].

In reality, the "curious old book written in Dutch", Agnos's "friend Michael Jelstra" and "Jan Svilt" never existed! During his research in Dutch archives, Michiel Koolbergen soon concluded that *The Queer Dutchman* could not contain the truth. For example, Koolbergen found out that the ship of "Jan Svilt", the VOC-ship *Geertruyd*, was not part of the homebound fleet of 1725. Agnos's book is great fun to read but has nothing to do with reality. In fact, *The Queer Dutchman* is an embellishment of *The Just Vengeance of Heaven Exemplify'd*, as the latter is an embellishment of *An Authentick Relation*! In an endnote of his book, Koolbergen wrote:

> In a telephone call (on 9 January 2002) C. Adler told that he had been in The Netherlands before the publication of *The Queer Dutchman* and had got interested in the history of the country, especially that of the VOC; based on the text of *The Just Vengeance of Heaven Exemplify'd* and after "some years of study to the VOC" he wanted to make "a good story", resulting in the fake journal of Jan Svilt. Adler admitted that Jan Svilt, Captain Dirk van Kloop, Bandino Frans and other persons mentioned in the journal are all artificial. The Dutch friend, Michael Jelstra, mentioned in the foreword, is artificial as well; moreover, the

---

[73] Koolbergen, *Ibid*, p.259 and Agnos, *The Queer Dutchman*, 1993, p.5.

Dutch book with mariner's tales from 1762 and the records of the meeting of the ship's council on the *Geertruyd* [in which "Jan Svilt" was sentenced to exile on Ascension – A.R[74].] do not exist in reality.[75]

Regrettably, many people – including scientific authors – thought that Peter Agnos had found the truth about the Dutch castaway. For example:

- in 1986 the Dutch historian H. von Saher, in his publication of a VOC-story, assumed the documents used by Peter Agnos to be some of the rare authentic documents about sex inside the VOC[76];

- in 1997 the British author Alan Day thought "Jan Svilt" to be genuine, as Day wrote in his book *St Helena, Ascension and Tristan da Cunha*. Day's book is volume 197 of the important *World Bibliographical Series*, volumes from the Oxford University, comprising listings of all the important documents of a geographical entity. Moreover, Alan Day mentioned *The Just Vengeance of Heaven Exemplify'd* but not the more reliable *An Authentick Relation*;

- in 1998 the American scientist Louis Crompton, expert on history of homosexuality, wrote a positive review of *The Queer Dutchman*. In that review Crompton wrote that some parts of Agnos's book "read like novelistic flashbacks added by the translator (M. Jelstra) or the compiler (Peter Agnos)" but he did not know that Jan Svilt and Michael Jelstra never existed[77].

---

[74] Agnos, *Ibid*, 1993, p.11.

[75] Koolbergen, *Ibid*, p.260.

[76] H. von Saher, in his book *Emmanuel Rodenburg, of wat er op het eiland Bali geschiedde toen de eerste Nederlanders daar in 1597 voet aan wal zetten*, 1986. In English the title reads "Emmanuel Rodenburg or what happened when the Dutch came to the island Bali for the first time, in 1597.

[77] See the Amazon Bookshop Review:

http://www.amazon.co.uk/exec/obidos/ASIN/0914018035/qid%3D1130414063/202-5225462-1879019 Interestingly, in 1998 Louis Crompton *knew* – as one of the doubtless very few people in the world -about the existence of both *An Authentick Relation* (1728) and the *Just Vengeance of Heaven Exemplify'd* (1730) but he did not know they had very different texts. Crompton also wrote that he could not be certain that Agnos's sources of the 18th century really existed.

CHAPTER 11. The Dutch East India Company (VOC): a short history

Foundation of the VOC (1602)

The VOC was founded in 1602. The abbreviation "VOC" stands for *Vereenigde Oostindische Compagnie* literally meaning "United East Indian Company"[78]. The word "united" will be understood, if one considers that the company tried to unite the commercial interests of two rival provinces, Holland and Zeeland, as well as the interests of rival towns inside those provinces. The word "united" can also be explained, if we go back to the years preceding the foundation of the VOC. From about the year 1585, the merchants of Holland and Zeeland were no longer welcome in Spanish and Portuguese ports, so Dutch merchants could no longer distribute the precious Asian products over northern Europe. In those days, the merchandise consisted mainly of spices, of which pepper was most important. The Dutch merchants started to realise that they either had to buy the precious products directly from Asian producers or had to pirate homebound Spanish and Portuguese ships. For those purposes, several companies were founded in a number of towns in Holland and Zeeland. The companies were generally set up for just one expedition. These "pre-companies", as historians would call them later, suffered from fierce competition, nationally and internationally. After some pressure from the *Staten-Generaal* (the Parliament of the United Provinces) and the mighty *raadspensionaris* - a sort of Prime Minister - Johan van Oldenbarneveldt of Holland and *stadholder* Prince Maurits of Orange, the pre-companies and cities started negations for a "united" East India Company, which finally became the VOC in 1602.

---

[78] My information for this chapter comes from the following Dutch books: Gaastra, F.S., *De geschiedenis van de VOC*, 1991, Jacobs, E.M., *De Vereenigde Oost-Indische Compagnie*, 1997, Doeke Roos, *Zeeuwen en de VOC*, 1988

Organisation of the VOC

The VOC was one of the first examples of a so-called "limited" company, with shareholders supplying the capital and sharing in the profit, while the commanders made the daily decisions. The shareholders could only lose the money they had invested in their shares, but nothing more, even if the company would go bankrupt. The possibilities for the shareholders to influence the company's policy were, by the way, extremely limited.

Its entire existence, the VOC consisted of six "chambers", notably the chambers of Zeeland (the entire province), Amsterdam (Holland), Delft (Holland), Rotterdam (Holland), Hoorn (Holland) and Enkhuizen (Holland). In total, there were 60 directors, of whom 20 came from the Chamber of Amsterdam. For most of them, the directorship was only a sideline job. Only a few directors had really knowledge of matters and dedicated enough time to leading the company. Some of the 60 directors were members of the top company's organization, the *Heeren Zeventien* (literally "Lords Seventeen"); the Chamber of Amsterdam appointed eight lords, the Chamber of Zeeland four, whereas the four other chambers appointed one lord each. The seventeenth lord was the chairman, who could be appointed by any Chamber except by that of Amsterdam. Obviously, this construction was chosen to prevent mighty Amsterdam from overruling the smaller chambers!

In the patent of 1602 (and later ones), the operating area of the VOC was officially defined as the area east of Cape of Good Hope and west of the Straits of Magellan. The VOC not only represented the Dutch *commercial* interests in that large area but also the *diplomatic* and *military* interests. On behalf of the *Staten-Generaal*, the VOC was allowed to enter into treaties with Asian kings and princes, to build fortresses, to appoint governors, to appoint judges and to equip armies. Although the VOC was primarily a matter of the provinces of Holland and Zeeland, the other five provinces of the United Provinces tried to keep some control over the VOC via the *Staten-Generaal*; after all, it was the *Staten-Generaal* of *all* provinces that granted the VOC its monopoly rights, which always had to be renewed after a certain number of years. However, the *Staten-Generaal* never deprived the VOC of its monopoly power[79].

The VOC as a colonial power

In the early 18th century the Dutch East Indies were quite extensive. The most important town of the Dutch East Indian colonies was Batavia (now Jakartra, the capital of Indonesia), built by the Dutch in the style of Amsterdam (with canals), with some 50,000 inhabitants. Other possessions of the VOC included towns and fortresses on Ceylon (now Sri Lanka), on the Malabar Coast (the west coast of what would later become British India) and on the Coromandel Coast (the east coast of what would later become British India). The most western outpost of the VOC was Capetown in modern South Africa, an obligatory resupply station for captains on both homebound and outbound voyages. Of course, the VOC employed thousands of people; for details, see the table at the end of this chapter.

The VOC as an employer

The VOC was by no means a good employer, certainly not for its lowest personnel. The sanitary situations on board the ships and in the tropical towns, barracks and fortresses were often abominable, causing many victims. For the general public, the best-known illness on board ships is scurvy, yet typhus probably caused more suffering and death. After arrival in an Asian town, many newcomers died as a result of tropical diseases:

> Yet there were those who, either in health or sickness, reached Batavia (or sometimes other Asiatic ports) and then died there before they could actually begin to discharge their duties. Disease contracted on board ship or in Batavia's exhausting climate must have claimed victims

---

[79] In early 1795 the United Provinces were overrun by French troops, whereas the English sacked many of the VOC-ships. Formally, the VOC ceased to exist on 3 December 1799, the date mentioned in the last granted patent. But by that time, the United Provinces did not exist any more, and the French puppet state, which had replaced the United Provinces (called the "Batavian Republic"), had virtually no naval and colonial power.

soon after arrival. In particular in the eighteenth century Batavia was a most unfavourable reception centre in this respect. The large town with its population crowded in a relatively small space became a dangerous hotbed of disease by pollution alone, partly due to the stagnant water in its canals. This danger applied particularly to the new arrivals who as yet had built up little resistance against tropical diseases, and had to get accustomed to the damp heat ashore, enveloping them like a clammy blanket[80].

An outbound VOC-ship started its voyage with an average of about 200 people on board. This was more than necessary for navigation purposes but the authorities always anticipated substantial losses caused by illness and death. Moreover, an outbound ship also housed many soldiers who would stay in the East for some time (often many years). Not very surprisingly, a *homebound* VOC-ship left the Asian port with an average of only about 100 people.

Throughout the entire period of the VOC (1602-1795) the salary structure for employees rarely changed. The following list gives an indication:

- soldier	9 guilders (a month)
- corporal (military)	14 guilders
- clerk (assistant bookkeeper)	16 guilders
- bookkeeper	22 guilders
- sailor	9 to 12 guilders
- under-merchant	about 40 guilders
- navigating officer on a ship	up to 50 guilders
- ship's captain	up to 80 guilders

---

[80] DAS 1978/1987, *Dutch-Asiatic shipping in the 17th and 18th centuries* under edition from J.R. Bruijn, F.S. Gaastra and I. Schoeffer, 1978/1987 (three parts), part 1, p.170.

The salaries for the lowest employees of the VOC, the soldiers and the sailors, were about the same as those of unschooled construction workers of that time. In some respects, a lower VOC-employee had a better job than a construction worker, because the latter had to pay for housing, food and drink. Moreover, the VOC-employee was sure of a long contract period, whereas the construction worker continually had to seek for new employment. However, the construction worker had a far better chance of staying alive for the years to come! Regarding the low salaries, the circumstances on board and in Asia and the high risk of not coming back - one in three did not return! -, one understands that most lower VOC-employees were men who had failed in finding jobs on shore, were single and came from the lowest classes. They often came from poor foreign countries; over the entire period of the VOC about 60% of the soldiers were foreigners and so were about 40% of the sailors! Not surprisingly, native Dutch were well represented in the better-paid VOC-jobs, such as under-merchant, navigating officer and ship's captain. Nonetheless, many experienced Dutch mariners preferred sailing in European waters, which was less risky and usually better paid than sailing in service of the VOC.

A man who started his VOC-career in the United Provinces, waiting to be shipped to Asia, frequently sailed out with a huge debt (often as much as 150 guilders[81]) to the dubious recruiter who had offered him his job and had arranged his housing until he was allowed on board.

A VOC-employee who was lucky enough to return in the United Provinces had some opportunities to enhance his modest salary by selling products that he had bought at low prices in Asia. Although the VOC-authorities partly allowed such private trade, they also strictly regulated it. The higher the function, the more chests were allowed and the larger the chests could be! Moreover, higher personnel in Asia had far better opportunities for private trade (not to speak of corruption) than lower personnel. Although the *Heeren Zeventien* tried to combat corruption, they were also guilty of corruption themselves. For example, the *Heeren Zeventien* and other VOC-VIPs in the United Provinces often appointed friends and family members (of course belonging to their "higher" classes) to positions with excellent opportunities for private trade. Such a

---

[81] For a soldier with a salary of 9 guilders a month, this was 17 months of salaries!

position was under-merchant[82] with a monthly salary of 40 guilders, an amount that a member of the upper class did not want to be dependent on. No problem, because once the under-merchant was in Asia he simply made dozens, if not hundreds, of guilders a month by private trade. Of course, the VOC was deprived of income sources this way but all control failed. Sometimes the *Heeren Zeventien* sent independent controllers to the East, directly responsible to the *Heeren Zeventien* and not to the local rulers in Asia. The controllers usually completely failed by counteraction of the VOC-personnel in Asia. Not very surprisingly, the controllers often became corrupt themselves.

The shipping routes of the VOC

Around 1600 the Dutch had to discover the routes to Asia that the Portuguese already knew. Moreover, the Dutch tried to sail to Asia via a Northeastern passage around Russia, which turned out to be impossible (although the Dutch found profitable whaling opportunities that way). One of the last discovery voyages of the VOC was the voyage of Abel Tasman in 1642-45, when he circumnavigated Australia (although he missed most of Australia's southern shores and all its eastern shores) and discovered parts of the coasts of Tasmania and New Zealand. Nowadays, Abel Tasman is regarded as a great explorer but in Tasman's days, the VOC-authorities at Batavia and the *Heeren Zeventien* were not amused about Tasman's discoveries. In their view, Tasman's voyage had cost a lot of money, without bringing in any new opportunities for the company's trade and profit!

By 1700 VOC-voyages between Europe and the Asian colonies had become routine. The captains had strict orders about the routes.

An outward voyage started at some roadstead in Holland or Zeeland, where the ships often had to wait for good departure conditions for weeks. Sometimes members of the crew already contracted contagious diseases. The ships from the Chamber of Zeeland started at the relatively good roadstead of Vlissingen[83] in the River Scheldt but departure could

---

[82] In Dutch *onderkoopman*

[83] In English this town is often called "Flushing"

only be done at daylight with eastern winds. Departure was preferably done at an outgoing tide, so that the ships did not have to sail against the stream. Perfect piloting was needed to avoid the dangerous banks in the mouth of the Scheldt[84]. Ships from the Chambers of Amsterdam, Hoorn and Enkhuizen first had to cross the shallow Zuyder Zee - nowadays called the Lake Yssel - with little cargo. Most cargo and crew members came on board at the roadstead of Oudeschild in the south of the island of Texel. Ships from the Chambers of Delft and Rotterdam had to make a long voyage through inland waters before reaching the roadstead of Goeree.

Once a VOC-ship was in the North Sea, she could reach the Atlantic Ocean via the English Channel or by sailing around Scotland. The route around Scotland was generally taken in times of war with England or France but also when southwestern winds hindered a passage through the English Channel.

Once a VOC-ship was in the Atlantic Ocean, the course was southwest. In the South Atlantic Ocean the ships had to sail parallel to the Brazilian shores, of course without getting too close to them. The tiny rocky islets of the Abrolhos were notoriously treacherous; indeed Abrolhos is Portuguese for "keep your eyes open"! On the outward voyage, the ships sailed hundreds of kilometres west of the islands of Ascension and Saint Helena, simply because of the prevailing southeastern trade winds. At around 40 degrees south, the prevailing westerly winds had to blow the ships to Capetown, an important resupply centre of the VOC.

After a compulsory stop at Capetown (sometimes more than a month), the prevailing westerly winds had to bring the VOC-ships in the direction of Australia. The ships had to head north at the right moment to reach Batavia; if the destination was not Batavia but one of the VOC-stations in Ceylon or India, that right moment came, of course, much earlier. As longitude could not be measured accurately in those days, the decision to head north was one of the most difficult decisions for the navigating officers. Regarding this fact, it is hardly surprising that Australia's west

---

[84] Doeke Roos, *Zeeuwen en de VOC*, pp.96-97

coast, including a group of coral islands called Abrolhos[85], is home to at least four and perhaps seven VOC-shipwrecks. If the ship did not run aground at the Australian coast, another problem often occurred if Strait Sunda (between the islands of Sumatra and Java) was not reached immediately. Very often, the ships reached the coasts of Sumatra to the west of Strait Sunda, from where it was often difficult to reach Batavia because of unfavourable winds.

For the navigating officers, the homeward voyages of the VOC-ships were not as difficult as the outward ones. From Batavia, India or Ceylon, Capetown could be reached in a straight line most of the time. From Capetown, the ships had to head in northwestern direction. When the ship was still close to Capetown, this could be a problem because of the winds but once the ship had reached the area of the southeast trade winds, it was easy. The ships often passed the island of Saint Helena and Ascension; both islands were sometimes used as rendezvous points. From Ascension, the ships were heading north and finally reached the United Provinces, either via the English Channel or via the waters north of Scotland. The route around Scotland was taken both in case of eastern winds in the English Channel and in case of war with Britain or France.

---

[85] The same (Portuguese) name as the rocky islets off Brazil! In chapter 13 an example of such a VOC-shipwreck (the *Zeewyk* in 1727-8) on the Abrolhos will be mentioned.

Personnel of the VOC outside the United Provinces (i.e. in Asia and Capetown, and on the ships) in three years in the 18th century

Category	1700	1753	1780
government, trade and justice	1026	1731	1506
Religion	95	172	148
health care	205	378	308
Craftsmen	1266	2253	1650
sea-going personnel	1375	3314	2881
Military	8923	11040	9173
Artillery	393	710	858
Various	201	503	643
Asian personnel	723	1724	
personnel on ships	3913	3054	1285
	18120	24879	18452

Source; F.S. Gaastra, *De geschiedenis van de VOC*, 1991, p.87

The table contains interesting information, although not everything is clear. For example, it looks odd to call "Asian personnel" a category, because those Asians must have been craftsmen, military or whatsoever. In 1780 there must have been Asian personnel but these individuals were not represented in the statistics. Moreover, the difference between "sea-going personnel" and "personnel on ships" is not clear. However, the table is reliable enough to draw some interesting conclusions. For example, if we take the categories "military" and "artillery" together, we have about fifty percent of the personnel in Asia, showing the enormous importance of the military presence of the VOC over there. In contrast, the category "government, trade and justice" represented less than 10 percent of the total number of employees.

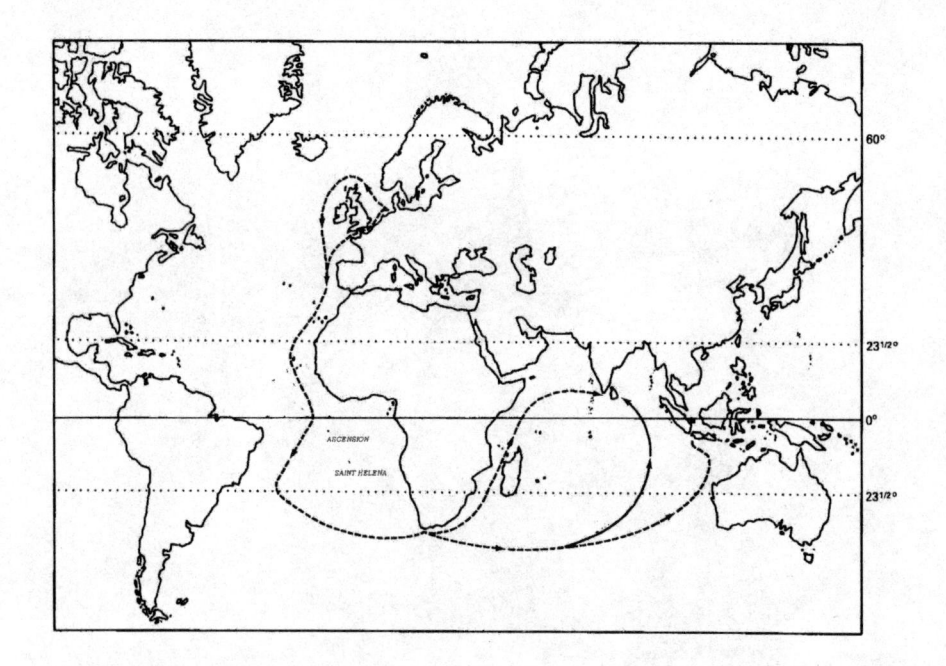

The outbound *routes of the VOC. The ships usually got close to the islands of Saint Helena and Ascension on the* homebound *routes only (from Koolbergen's book, slightly adjusted)*

The flag of the VOC: the "A" stands for the Chamber of Amsterdam (drawing by Anneke de Vries, from a photo by the author of the VOC-ship Amsterdam *in the Amsterdam Maritime Museum).*

A VOC-ship of the 18th century (drawing by Anneke de Vries, from a photo by the artist herself of the VOC-ship Amsterdam *in the Amsterdam Maritime Museum)*

CHAPTER 12. The VOC and the "detestable crime of sodomy"

In the 18th century, sodomy was considered a very serious crime in the United Provinces, as a result of religious – Calvinistic - fanaticism. To begin with, we should realise that in the early 18th century the term "homosexuality" did not yet exist, neither in Dutch nor in other languages. In those days the Dutch used the word *sodomie* as a collective term for all sexual activities not related to procreation, such as sexual activities between people of the same sex, sex with animals and even masturbation. Sometimes *sodomie* only applied to effeminate behaviour by men. In the Dutch language of the early 18th century there were also other – rather euphemistic - expressions for sodomy, such as (translated into modern English), "the stupid sin", "sodomitic obscenities" and "unnatural acts".

The death penalty was applicable for "full sodomy", meaning anal intercourse with ejaculation inside the body. Especially during the early 18th century Dutch judges did not distinguish between "active" and "passive" sodomy, not even if the "passive" partner had been raped[86]. When "full sodomy" could not be proven, the prisoner got a lesser punishment, for which every judge had a large degree of discretion. Mutual masturbation was considered a crime as well but not a capital one; offenders were punished by imprisonment, banishment or corporal punishment.

Around 1730 the roundups, trials and executions of sodomites reached a peak in the United Provinces. In the spring of that year Dutch authorities rounded up sodomite networks in the towns of Amsterdam and Utrecht. In both towns many men were executed, imprisoned or banished. As a result, on 21 July 1730 the *Staten-Generaal* (the Dutch Parliament) issued new legislation against sodomy. From that moment, Dutch judges were

---

[86] The Dutch legislation followed Leviticus 20:13, where the death penalty is demanded for both active and passive sodomy, see the *King James Bible* : "If a man also lie with mankind, as he lieth with a woman, both of them have committed an abomination: they shall surely be put to death; their blood shall be upon them."

compulsed to pronounce death sentences for "full sodomy". Interestingly, the legislation of 1730 demanded the *public* execution of sodomites, whereas earlier death penalties for sodomy had usually been executed between closed walls. Between 1730 and 1732 more than 300 people were prosecuted for sodomy in the United Provinces, of which at least 75 were punished by death, including 22 boys and men who were strangled and subsequently burnt in the village of Faan in the province of Groningen on 24 September 1731, after an extraordinary trial[87].

Not surprisingly, the authorities of the VOC and other shipping companies tried to prevent sodomy on board their ships. For that reason, the food on board of VOC-ships included generous dosages of saltpetre, which was supposed to "cool the flesh" and reduce the men's urges towards unnatural acts[88]. Of course, the ship's authorities also severely punished sodomy, already long before the legislation of 1730. For example, in 1707 five sailors were drowned in the roadsted of Texel Island for sodomy[89].

In 1988 the Dutch historian Tecla Aerts wrote an excellent paper about the prosecution of sodomy inside the VOC[90]. For her article, Aerts studied all 18th century trials of sodomy that she could find in the jurisdictional archives of the VOC in Capetown, a town and resupply station ruled by the VOC. Most trials in Capetown referred to cases that had taken place on board VOC-ships, because the ship's councils often handed over criminal cases to the authorities in the next harbour town, which was often Capetown. Tecla Aerts found 44 legal cases between 1700 and 1794: almost 150 persons were involved, as culprits, accomplices or victims. Nine persons were sentenced to death. Many culprits were sentenced to forced labour on Robben Island off Capetown.

---

[87] Meer, T. van der, *Sodoms zaad in Nederland*, 1995, p.18

[88] Hugh Edwards, *The Wreck on the Half-Moon Reef*, page 38.

[89] Meer, T. van der, *Ibid*, p.26

[90] Tecla Aerts, *Het verfoeilijke crime van sodomie*, in Leidschrift, April 1988, pp.5-21

In her article, Aerts called the community of a VOC-ship an example of a "total institution"[91], i.e. an institution characterised by strong rules, a strict hierarchical structure, little or no contact with members of the opposite sex and a lack of privacy. Inside the communities of total institutions (ships, prisons, armies, cloisters, boarding schools and so on), homosexual contacts are often far more frequent than in the outer world. In many, if not most, homosexual contacts inside a total institution, a higher person seduces or rapes a lower one.

By studying the various cases, Aerts found out that most seductions and rapes took place at the few spots on board where one could not be caught *in flagrante delicto* immediately: below decks, in the sleeping areas, in the lavatories, in the long-boat, at the look-out post, and so on. Officers often had private cabins and hence they had better opportunities to commit the "stupid sin". The records of the trials mention many methods that the seducers used to attract partners, from offering money and pipes to intimidation. In court, the accused never mentioned a homosexual inclination to explain their acts; in many cases they blamed the alcohol or the Devil.

Regarding the strict hierarchical situation on board the ships, it is hardly surprising that Aerts found out that in most sexual contacts the "active" man was higher in rank, older and more experienced than the "passive" man, the latter often being a boy. The higher-ranked man often had no problems in intimidating the lower-ranked one. For example, in 1746 first officer Twist threatened a boy, that if he would pass on something, he would be thrown overboard in a bag. In 1753 one Anthonij van Malta threatened a boy that both he and the boy would face the death penalty if their case would be brought to justice[92].

In fact, the higher-ranked men threatening the lower-ranked ones were right, because – especially in the early 18th century - Dutch judges on both land and sea did not distinguish between active sodomy and passive sodomy. As a result, in case of a rape the judges punished offender and

---

[91] Aerts followed the American sociologist Erving Goffman, who invented the term "total institution".
[92] T.M.Aerts, *Ibid*, p17.

victim to the same degree. For example, in 1725 VOC-judges in Capetown dealt with the case of a 25-year old sailor, who had raped an 18-year old slave. Both were found guilty and drowned, bound back to back. Similar things could happen if someone had sex with an animal, as is shown by a case in 1764. In that year one Jan Hantszoon van Eleveld was sentenced for having had sodomy with a pig while he was drunk. The pig was killed and the man was flogged, branded and banished to Robben Island for the rest of his life. One year later he was sentenced for having raped a sheep. This time, he was thrown into the sea, with the sheep bound around his neck.

There are examples of boys who were found guilty of "full sodomy" but escaped the death sentence because of their age. However, there was no general Dutch rule about the minimum age for a prisoner to be applicable to the death penalty. Here are a few examples of boys who were punished for sodomy.

In 1731, in the village of Faan in the province of Groningen, a trial for sodomy lead to the public execution of twenty-two men and boys, including nine boys aged fifteen to eighteen. However, the harsh judge decided to exclude two fourteen-year old boys from the death penalty; they had to watch the executions and were sent to jail for the rest of their lives[93].

In 1746 the court at the Cape of Good Hope tried a cabin boy from the VOC for sodomy. In court, he astonished his judges by stating that he had done it with his brother, and that his brother had done it with him, not realising he had done something that was considered a capital crime. The boy was sentenced to 25 years of forced labour on Robben Island, although the public prosecutor had advocated life imprisonment.

---

[93] Van der Meer, *Ibid*, p.145. All the other examples of sodomy in this chapter are derived from the article of Tecla Aerts, *Ibid*. For excellent information, written in English, about the mania against sodomy in the United Provinces around 1730 (including the massacre at Faan in Groningen), see http://www.gayhistory.com/rev2/events/1730.htm Van der Meer has an interesting website, see http://www.iisg.nl/staff/tvm.php .

In 1751, in the province of Utrecht, four sixteen-year old boys were arrested for a number of crimes, including having formed a sodomite network. The Court of Utrecht judged two of the four boys and considered them too young to understand the seriousness of their crime. The two boys were whipped and sent to a cloister near Aachen in Germany. However, the two other boys were judged by the court of the village of Zeist and were sentenced to death. The latter two boys were finally strangled, in spite of efforts of the Court of Utrecht to save their lives[94].

Leendert Hasenbosch was not the only Dutchman who was banished to a desert island for sodomy. On 2 December 1727, two and a half years after the exile of Hasenbosch, the council of the VOC-ship *Zeewyk* sentenced two boys to exile for having committed sodomy together. By that time, the *Zeewyck* had been wrecked on one of the islands of the Houtman Abrolhos, off the west coast of Australia. The crew had been living for months on one of the larger islands of the Abrolhos. So the boys were sentenced to be marooned for acts committed while they were marooned. The official sentence of the two boys is quite indicative, containing a mixture of religious arguments and the wish to set an example[95];

> Inasmuch as following the accusation of 2 quartermasters and a seaman of the Company's late ship *Zeewyk*, now wrecked off the islands named by us Frederik Houtmans, with regard to the persons named Adriaen Spoor, van St. Maertensdyck, junior seaman; and Pieter Engels van Ghent, junior seaman; of the complement of the ship mentioned. It appeared to us clearly and truthfully that the persons mentioned, on 30th November, 1727, at about 3 o'clock in the afternoon, committed in the island the abominable and God-forsaken deeds of Sodom and Gomorrah, to the great sorrow of the officers, distress of the crew, and general peril on our island. Through which deed terrible plagues may strike our people, or discord may occur among us, with the loss of all that is good. The outrageous and God-forsaken manner of living has reached such a height that the junior seamen did not fear God nor justice in committing the acts. Inasmuch as three persons named Frans Feban, quartermaster, Dirck van Griecken, quartermaster, and

---

[94] Van der Meer, *Ibid*, p.145.
[95] Hugh Edwards, *Ibid*, pp.100-105

Hendrick Armanse, seaman, present in this island by accident happened to find these junior seamen doing these abominable deeds. All of which are of a dangerous and evil nature and where justice prevails ought to be punished by death for the prevention of further evil.

Therefore the full Council of the island mentioned resolved with the greatest speed to place burning fuses between the fingers of those persons to make them confess. But they, being obdurate, refused to confess. Whereupon we have resolved in council to place them apart from each other in the remotest islands. Which decision has been unanimously reached and approved and have had the junior seamen conveyed to the islands in the yawl on the 2nd day of December, anno 1727. This verdict has been passed, sentenced, announced, and executed by us at Frederik Houtman, on December 2nd 1727.

We know the names of the two unfortunate boys - Adriaen Spoor and Pieter Engels - but we do not know their ages. The two boys were marooned, each on a separate island. The log of the *Zeewyk* describes the transportation of the two boys by a longboat but does not mention whether the boys were supplied with food and water; most likely, the boys were not. The boys must have been marooned on the islands nowadays called Mangrove Islands, being only coral slates reaching only about a metre above the high water line. As the islands have neither water nor food, the two boys must have died in a terrible way. Unlike Leendert Hasenbosch, the two boys of the *Zeewyk* were not granted a survival chance at all. For them, their sentence to exile was a virtual death sentence.

CHAPTER 13. The marooning of Leendert Hasenbosch, compared with other maroonings around 1700

Around 1700, as in our time, stories and legends of castaways on desert islands were very popular. Of course, the most famous story is Daniel Defoe's *Robinson Crusoe*, first published in 1719. Many contemporaries believed Robinson Crusoe to be genuine, because Defoe's name was not on the book and the title page stated that the story had been written by Robinson Crusoe himself. Robinson Crusoe came upon his fictitious desert island as a result of a shipwreck in a terrible storm. The only survivors were Crusoe, a dog and two female cats. It was a most unusual shipwreck, because Crusoe could salvage incredibly many artefacts, such as Dutch cheeses, good muskets and pistols with plenty of ammunition, clothes, bibles and prayer books, paper, pens and ink, seaman's chests, ropes and sails, etc The island provided Crusoe with plenty of fresh water. He had salvaged many seeds from the wreck, providing him many good harvests over the years. In fact, Crusoe's life was never endangered by lack of food or water. Of course, the lives of *real* castaways were never as easy and romantic as that of Crusoe, as Edward E. Leslie wrote in *Desperate Journeys, Abandoned Soles*:

> Possessed of such wealth, (...) many another real maroon might well have been reluctant to give up a life in seclusion to return to the risks and poverty of the sailor's trade.
>
> Of course, Daniel Defoe and most of the old masters of survival literature were not attempting to draw an entirely factual portrait of a maroon's predicament. Quite the contrary – for them the island experience was an allegory of the human condition, and they used it to show the psychological transformation of their protagonists. Thus they relieved them of the true and desperate burdens of elemental existence in order to work to an internal alteration. Given the time, in other words, to meditate and remember, the fictional characters undergo profound change[96].

---

[96] Edward E. Leslie, *Desperate Journeys, Abandoned Souls*, 1988, pp.63-64

Between 1697 and 1725 the stories of three *real* castaways were published in the English language:

- the Mosquito Indian Will on Juan Fernandez Island[97] between 1681 and 1684. The story of his marooning and rescue was included in William Dampier's book *A New Voyage round the World*, first published in 1697;

- the Scotchman Alexander Selkirk (1680-1721) on Juan Fernandez Island between 1704 and 1709. The story of his solitary life and rescue were immortalised by his rescuer Woodes Rogers, in his book *A Cruising Voyage Round the World* (first published in 1712) and by journalist Richard Steele in an article in the newspaper *The Englishman* dated 1 December 1713[98]. According to many experts, the stories of Will and – especially - Selkirk inspired Defoe for the writing of *Robinson Crusoe*;

- the North-American (from the British colonies that would later become the USA) Philip Ashton, who stayed utterly alone on Roatan Island for sixteen months, in 1723-24. After he had come home, Ashton himself wrote the *History of the Strange Adventures and Signal Deliverances of Mr. Philip Ashton*, published in Boston in 1725[99].

Will and Selkirk stayed on the main island of the archipelago of Juan Fernandez, located in the Pacific Ocean, at about 34 degrees southern

---

[97] In those days Juan Fernandez Island was the name for the largest island of the archipelago of the same name. Until 1966 the official name of the main island was *Más-á-tierra* (Spanish for "Nearer Land"). In January 1966 the Chilean authorities officially renamed it *Isla Robinson Crusoe*. Near the island's western tip we find a much smaller island, Santa Clara, although it was also often called Goat Island. The third island of the archipelago is about half as large as the main island and is located 150 kilometres to the west. The third island used to be called *Mas Afuera* (Spanish for "Further Away"), until in January 1966 it was officially renamed *Isla Alejandro Selkirk* – although Selkirk never was on that island! Nowadays, the largest island is the only inhabited one and has some 500 inhabitants, living from agriculture, fisheries (especially of *langostas* or lobster-sized crayfish) and eco-tourism.

[98] Strictly spoken, there was also a fourth source, Edward Cook, *A Voyage to the South Sea, and Around the World* (1712), which is not very informative. All sources for the stories of Will and Selkirk are on website:

http://academic.brooklyn.cuny.edu/english/melani/novel_18c/defoe/selkirk.html#dampier..

[99] For more details about the adventures of Philip Ashton, see Leslie, *Ibid*, pp.86-110 and Charles Neider, *Great Shipwrecks and Castaways; Authentic Accounts of Adventures at Sea*, 2000, pp.99-120.

latitude, some 600 kilometres west of the west coast of Chile. The island has a maximum length of 19 kilometres and a size of about 55 square kilometres. As the island had plenty of fresh water and fresh food, it is not surprising that around 1700 the island was often used as a resupply station by privateers harassing the rich Spanish colonies on the west coast of South America. Both Will and Selkirk were members of such privateering expeditions.

Philip Ashton stayed on Roatan Island off the Caribbean coast of Honduras, some fifty kilometres long and six kilometres wide. The island is quite hilly and has many rain forests[100].

Let us have a closer look at the adventures of Will, Selkirk, Ashton and Hasenbosch, focusing on their personalities, how they got marooned and how they tried to survive.

a) The personalities of the castaways

Will was an Indian of the Mosquito tribe from what is now Nicaragua or Honduras. In 1680 Will and some other Mosquitoes joined a group of English buccaneers to fight against the Spanish, their common enemy. As the Mosquitoes had no names of their own and we know Will and the other Mosquitoes by the names that their English comrades gave them. We do not know the year of birth of Will but in 1680 he was probably not yet old.

Selkirk was born in the Scottish village of Largo in 1680[101]. We know much more about Selkirk than about Will, Ashton or Hasenbosch. Selkirk grew up in a strong Calvinistic – or Presbyterian - society. As a teenager Selkirk was cited for misbehaviour in church and ran away to sea. Selkirk's character could be depicted as a "sea dog". His character was well described by Edward E. Leslie in *Desperate Journeys, Abandoned Soles*:

---

[100] Nowadays, Roatan Island has some 2,000 inhabitants and an important tourist industry.

[101] Diana Souhami, *Selkirk's Island*. (2001), p.80. Selkirk was born in 1680 but many authors put the birth year on 1676.

A difficult man was Alexander Selkirk. Much given to the vices of sailors - strong drink, loose women and brawling – he had a personality perfectly suited to such diversions: impulsive and hot-tempered with little respect for authority, quick to speak his mind and just as quick to fight.

Still, despite these traits, he was a skilful, hard-working mariner.[102]

In 1704, aged 23 or 24, Selkirk became quartermaster of an English ship on a private expedition against France and Spain. It was this expedition that would end in his solitary stay on Juan Fernandez.

The truth of Philip Ashton's solitary stay was sometimes doubted; his book would only be a novel inspired by *Robinson Crusoe*. However, unlike Crusoe, Ashton really existed. He was born in Marblehead in 1702, married twice and fathered six children. Ashton got marooned on Roatan Island when he was aged 20 or 21.

Hasenbosch was aged about 30 when he was banished to Ascension in 1725. He never was a mariner but followed a military career at the Dutch East India Company. He finally became the bookkeeper of the ship that was supposed to bring him home. For some ten years, Hasenbosch must have worn uniforms almost every day. Like Selkirk, Hasenbosch was probably a god-fearing Calvinist. Hasenbosch was probably of homosexual inclination, in a time that terms as "homosexuality" and "gay" did not yet exist.

b) How they got marooned

When Will and Selkirk made land on Juan Fernandez, they did not yet know they would become castaways. Both Will and Selkirk stayed on the island with their comrades for some time, for refreshment after long and dangerous journeys. Will was accidentally left behind. He was hunting for goats in the interior of the island and suddenly saw his comrades departing in haste, because of an attack by Spanish ships. Selkirk was left

---

[102] Leslie, *Ibid*, p.65.

behind because he refused to go on board again, having lost confidence in both his captain and the seaworthiness of his ship.

Ashton got marooned in a completely different way. When he was on board a schooner, that schooner was taken by pirates under the command of Edward (or Ned) Low, on 15 June 1722. Ashton refused to join the pirates. In early March 1723 the pirates anchored off Roatan Island and Ashton managed to escape to that desolate island[103].

Of the four castaways, Hasenbosch was the only one to be marooned by force, as a punishment for sodomy.

c) *How they survived*

When he was marooned, Will only had a gun, a knife, a small horn of powder and a few bullets. After the bullets were gone, he used his gun to make harpoons, a long knife and fishing hooks. He ate seals, goats and fish. He later killed seals only for their hides; he made fishing lines from those hides. His little hut, about one kilometre from the sea, was covered with goatskins. For clothing, he only wore a goatskin around his waist. When he was finally rescued by a new group of English buccaneers he killed three goats and served them up in the English fashion with cabbage from the cabbage-trees!

When Selkirk started his solitary life, he had many useful things, including clothes, bedding, a firelock, powder, bullets, tobacco, a hatchet, a knife, a kettle, a bible and other books. He is said to have built two huts from piemento trees and to have covered them with grass and goats skins. However, one of his huts might have been built by Will more than 20 years before.

Selkirk ate fish, crawfish and goat meat (broiled or boiled) but in the beginning he had problems eating without salt and bread. After some

---

[103] Ashton was listed in the *Boston News-Letter* of 9 July 1722, as being one of those captured by Edward Low (Leslie, *Ibid*, pp.107-108)

time, Selkirk managed to prepare his meals tastefully, with the many plants on the island: cabbage, fruits of the piemento trees, a black pepper and turnips. The turnips had been sown by William Dampier's men some years earlier.

Selkirk's shoes wore out after some time, forcing him to walk barefooted. The skin on his feet became so hard that he could run over the rocks without feeling pain. He learnt how to hunt goats on his feet, without a fire arm. When his clothes fell apart he clothed himself in goatskins. He even managed to make some shirts, from linen cloth and his useless socks.

Selkirk tamed goats and cats to have some company. His cats protected him from the rats that had caused him serious problems in the beginning.

Of the four castaways, Ashton was the only one to start with no equipment at all. Although there was plenty of wood on Roatan Island, he could not make a fire to cook a meal. As he had no knife or any other weapon, he could not kill any of the many hogs, deer or tortoises. In the beginning he seems to have survived on fruits and raw eggs only. Moreover, the numerous insects caused serious problems. Ashton built some huts but they did not protect him from the insects. After a few months he decided to cross the sea to a small offshore islet, although Ashton was not a good swimmer and only had some bamboo as a primitive raft. Moreover, at sea alligators and sharks could attack him. The windswept offshore islet was free of insects but Ashton often had to return to the main island for food and drink.

Ashton's situation changed to the better with the arrival of an Englishman, who had lived for twenty-two years among the Spanish and was now in flight from them because they had threatened to burn him for some unspecified reason. The two men lived together for two days, then the Englishman went away for a short time but Ashton never saw him again. Ashton was alone again but the Englishman had left behind "five pounds of pork, a knife, a bottle of gunpowder, tobacco, tongs, and flint"[104], making his life easier. He could now make fires, kill tortoises and catch crayfish and broil or roast meals.

Poor Hasenbosch! In contrast to Juan Fernandez and Roatan, Ascension was a dry and barren island, causing Hasenbosch to be in constant want for drinking water and firewood. Moreover, Ascension had virtually no edible plants except the local purslane.

Hasenbosch started his exile with a survival kit comparable to the kit of Selkirk. Among other things, Hasenbosch had clothes, a knife, a teakettle, a hatchet, one or more bibles or prayer books and drinking water for about a month. He even had some seeds but his gardening experiments failed. Once he had found the source of water we call Dampier's Drip nowadays, he probably thought to have found *the* island's spring, which was, however, hidden in the higher regions. He was obsessed with the lack of water until the end, forcing him to drink his own urine, sometimes mixed with the blood of turtles and birds.

In fact, Will and Selkirk had only one problem that Hasenbosch did not have. Hasenbosch would have welcomed any ship calling at his island but Will and Selkirk feared their Spanish enemies who would kill, imprison or enslave them. Selkirk seems to have been seen by the Spanish one time and Will even two or more times. Of course, the Spanish landings caused perilous situations for the castaways. If we may believe the renowned account of Rogers in *A Cruising Voyage Round the World*, Selkirk was hiding in the top of a tree while some of his Spanish enemies were pissing at the bottom of that tree! According to the same source, Selkirk would have surrendered if his enemies had been French instead of Spanish, because he knew the French would treat him humanely, as a prisoner of war. When Ashton was on his island, his country was not at war with Spain. However, when members of a Spanish landing party saw Ashton, he decided to fly into the interior of his island, probably because he expected that the Spanish would not treat him very well.

---

[104] Leslie, *Ibid*, p.101

The stories of Will and Selkirk became famous but they did not write down their stories themselves. Will could probably not write. Selkirk could write but he seems to have had no writing materials. Moreover, it is questionable whether a "sea dog" like Selkirk would have kept a diary if he had been able to do so. Ashton wrote down his adventures himself but he did so in retrospect; Ashton definitely had no writing materials on his island. However, Hasenbosch kept a diary, just as the fictitious and hence immortal Robinson Crusoe. Hasenbosch never knew that his exile would become a legend and that his diary would become a source of income for rewriters and publishers.

Selkirk has been called the *real* British Robinson Crusoe for more than two centuries, although Selkirk was a Scottish sea dog and Robinson Crusoe was an English gentleman. Selkirk will forever stay the real British Robinson Crusoe and Leendert Hasenbosch will forever be called the real Dutch one!

The rescue of the Mosquito Indian Will on 22 March 1684, after a solitary stay of more than three years. The first to greet him was another Mosquito Indian, Robin. William Dampier wrote that Robin "threw himself flat on his face at his feet, who helping him up, and embracing him, fell flat with his face on the Ground at Robin's feet, and was by him taken up also." (from Koolbergen's book)

The rescue of Alexander Selkirk, after a solitary stay of more than four years, on 1 February 1709 (12 February on the modern calendar, strictly spoken it was 1 February 1708/9 for the British) (from Koolbergen's book).

EPILOGUE. Another Dutchman on Ascension

I once saw a tourist brochure "Ascension Island is like nowhere else on earth". I can only say that the statement is very appropriate indeed. Although Ascension has been inhabited since 1815, yet there have never been "Ascensonians", because nobody has ever lived there permanently. All persons who have ever been allowed to live on Ascension were or are employed by one of the companies operating on the island, such as Cable and Wireless Limited, the Royal Air Force and the United States Air Force. Only some employees were (and are) allowed to live with their families on the island. As a result, the island houses relatively few children and no retired people at all. Of the present population of about 1,100, about 750 are "Saint Helenians" or "Saints", about 200 from the United Kingdom and about 150 from the United States.

The political status of Ascension is extremely complicated. Officially, Ascension is a dependency of the island of Saint Helena, some 1,200 kilometres to the southeast; Saint Helena, in its turn, is a dependency of the United Kingdom. The highest "boss" of Ascension is the Administrator. All tourists and other visitors still need his permission to land on the island. To make things even more complex, the island's airport is run by officials of both the United Kingdom and the United States. As late as 2002, Ascension got its first democratically elected council.

For tourist visits, Ascension was not opened until the late 1980s. The few tourists can enjoy themselves with game fishing, diving, mountain walking, bird and dolphin watching and golf. The Ascension golf course was once in the Guinness Book of Records as the worst golf course on earth. Georgetown, the main village, has a few interesting buildings, including some forts with guns. The surrounding sea has many undertows, so swimming in the sea is safe in only a few places. There are enjoyable bars in the villages and in the American base near the airport.

Ascension's airport was built for military reasons during the Second World War. Nowadays, the airport is still closed to civil aircraft. During most weeks, military and civilians can reach Ascension twice by planes of the Royal Air Force from Brize Norton, a military airport near Swindon in southern England. In fact, the airplanes use Ascension as a refuelling station on their journeys between the Falkland Islands and Brize Norton. Apart from the RAF, there is only one way of public transport to Ascension: a cruise on the Royal Mail Ship *Saint Helena* that has regular services between Ascension and Saint Helena (travel time: two days, about 20 connections in each direction a year) and between Saint Helena and Capetown (travel time: five days, about 20 connections in each direction a year). The RMS *Saint Helena* is a "must" especially for Saint Helena, because that island (inhabited by about 5,000 "Saints") does not have an airport. In other words, Saint Helena has even fewer connections with the outside world than Ascension.

At present (early 2006) an airport is under construction on Saint Helena that should be ready around 2010. Hopefully, the airport on Ascension will be open to civil aircraft by that time. In that case, there will hopefully be some tourist development on both islands, although they will – and should – never become tourist meccas as Mallorca, Gran Canaria, Bermuda or the Bahamas. I hope Ascension and Saint Helena will get some skilfully managed ecotourism, comparable with the Brazilian island of Fernando de Noronha, which I visited on another holiday. Both Ascension and Saint Helena are rich in nature and historic buildings and offer excellent opportunities for hiking, game fishing, diving and more. And last but not least, both islands have a friendly English-speaking population; although, as I wrote before, Ascension has never had a "real" population.

I visited Saint Helena and Ascension during a long holiday in July and August 2000. I first took a plane from Amsterdam to Capetown, stayed a few days in Capetown, stayed five nights on the RMS *Saint Helena*, stayed a week in a flat on Saint Helena, stayed two more nights on the RMS *Saint Helena* and disembarked at Ascension. I stayed ten days on Ascension and left with the RAF.

A cruise on the RMS *Saint Helena* is a unique experience. Compared to other cruise ships, the RMS *Saint Helena* is a small ship, with only about 100 crewmembers and a maximum capacity of 130 passengers. Most of the approximately 100 crewmembers are from Saint Helena but most officers are from the UK. Roughly, the passengers can be divided into "Saints" and "Non-Saints". Most of the "Non-Saints" can roughly be divided into cruise passengers and people who need to be on Saint Helena for professional reasons. For example, on my trip there were a biologist, a businessman, a journalist and some British officials on board. Most members of the last group embarked at Capetown, stayed a week on Saint Helena and disembarked at Ascension. Most cruise passengers also stayed a week on Saint Helena, although a few stayed on the RMS *Saint Helena* while she was "shuttling" between the two islands. In fact, most tourist accommodations on Saint Helena are only used those days that coincide with the schedule of the RMS *Saint Helena*.

On 10 August 2000, on board the RMS *Saint Helena*, I got my first glimpse of Ascension Island. It was bright weather, with the island's summit free of clouds, and Ascension Frigate Birds (*Fregata aquila*) circling high above the ship; I had seen the first frigate bird about one hour before I saw the island. I had not expected those birds would venture out so far, because of a remarkable characteristic of this large and beautiful seabird: in contrast to other seabirds frigate birds cannot swim!

How luxurious was my welcome to Ascension compared to that of Leendert Hasenbosch on 5 May 1725! I already knew that I would stay overnight in the guesthouse. I knew I would buy the *Ascension Island Walks Book* in the tourist office. I knew that I would leave on 20 August with the RAF. I was looking forward to wearing my mountain boots again and explore the island, with its funny place names as Deadman's Beach, Comfortless Cove, Breakneck Valley, Spoon Crater, Lady Hill, Devil's Ashpit, Devil's Riding School and Devil's Cauldron. There are no goats on the island any more but there are many sheep and donkeys.

I explored Ascension as I had explored Saint Helena and other islands; on my mountain boots! Ascension's high interior is lushly green, in contrast to the dry and bleak coastal regions with their dark volcanic rocks. On the island's summit we find a small pond, called Dew Pond, surrounded by so many bamboo trees that you have no view from there; of course, there are enough excellent view points from other high locations. However, virtually *all* trees and other vegetation have been imported, leaving less place for the scarce but endemic – i.e. unique - vegetation of the island. Just below the island's top we find an abandoned farm with several neglected patches and buildings, once important for the island's food supply but nowadays virtually all food is simply imported. From the farm, an impressive man-made tunnel creates an important shortcut to another valley.

A highlight of my stay on Ascension was a boat trip around Boatswain Bird Island, Ascension's "satellite" with an area of some five hectares. Hundreds of seabirds are breeding on Boatswain Bird Island during all months of the year. "Boatswain Bird" is the local name for the sea bird species officially called "tropicbird"[105]. Ascension has two species of these beautiful birds, one with a red bill (*Phaeton aethereus*) and a smaller one with a yellow bill (*Phaeton lepturus*). Boatswain Bird Island and the many stacks around Ascension are paradises for seabirds; on many spots the dark volcanic rocks turn white because of the birds and their droppings! Prior to about 1815, the main island itself was a paradise for seabirds as well but after the arrival of the first colonists most seabirds vanished due to rats, cats and dogs.

At present (early 2006), the dogs have long gone and all wild cats have been recently exterminated. The people may only hold neutered and "permanently chipped" cats; of course, these measures were taken to let the seabirds return to the main island. Other projects have started to restore the indigenous vegetation.

The only seabird species that continued to breed in large numbers after the arrival of the cats is the Sooty Tern (*Sterna fuscata*), locally called Wideawake Tern. The official name of the island's airport is Wideawake Airport, located close to one of the breeding colonies. The cats could not exterminate this species, because the birds have a ten-month-breeding cycle and so they are away from the island for two months a year, leading to an extraordinary balance between the numbers of preys and predators!

When I was on Ascension I had already read the excellent book by Duff Hart-Davis, *Ascension, the story of a South Atlantic island*. Thanks to Hart-

---

[105] Sometimes local names of places, animals and plants are quite different from the official ones. For example, on Saint Helena the name is "trophybird"! I had been watching the red-billed species on Saint Helena already. I had similar experiences in holidays in Ireland and Scotland!

Davis's book I knew the legend of the Dutch castaway on Ascension of 1725 but during my stay I did not think of him. To be honest, I doubted whether the entire marooning had ever occurred. I did not know that a few years before another Dutchman, Michiel Koolbergen, had visited Ascension in order to disclose the truth. I visited Dampier's Cave, not knowing it had – probably - been the habitat of the castaway. In his book, Michiel Koolbergen stated that Dampier's Cave should better be named Dutchman's Cave and I think he was quite right.

Here are a few entertaining – translated - passages from Michiel Koolbergen's book, in which he described his visit to Ascension, possibly in the year 1996[106];

> (….) An old hospital was rebuilt into a luxurious residence [for the Administrator – A.R.], including a bar in the garden, where one, as a guest, soon forgets the sad look of Georgetown. "Now, tell me, did that Dutch castaway exist or not", the Administrator [Roger Huxley – A.R.] asked me during an animated conversation with a beer, for he had, like others on Ascension, heard about the story, not in the least thanks to the fake story by the American Cyrus Adler alias Peter Agnos. And I assured him that Agnos's book was no more than a fake story, although there had been a real Dutch castaway indeed. When I also stated that the castaway's name had to stay a secret for some time but that my book about the subject would have the title "A Dutch Robinson Crusoe", he nodded in agreement. (…)
>
> On Ascension, I met the man who had lived there the longest and knew most of the history of Ascension. On the evening of a weekday we walked along a two-storey building, not far from the sea, the highest storey housing the Exiles Club. The bar was closed but Graham Avis, as a member, had a key (….)
>
> (….) Graham Avis, an expert on the history and legends of Ascension, had, of course, heard about the Dutch castaway. When he had studied my copy of the diary of the Dutch Robinson Crusoe, he was immediately willing to go on a two-day search with me. With his Land Rover – the favourite means of transport on Ascension – we drove to the spots on the island that seemed to fit the descriptions that the Dutch Robinson Crusoe gave in the diary in 1725. The visit to the cave that was his dwelling for some time, called Dampier's Cave, was a

---

[106] Information given to me by Graham Avis. In his book, Michiel Koolbergen did not mention the dates of his visit to Ascension.

special adventure. The cave on the Caribbean island of Tobago where Robinson supposedly had lived was tourist nonsense. The cave on the Chilean Robinson Crusoe Island, where Alexander Selkirk, the real Robinson Crusoe, allegedly had lived was fake. But this cave on Ascension was truly the cave in which the Dutch Robinson Crusoe had sought his refuge for some time. I searched for an inscripted message on the walls, something like "Hasenbosch was here"; in vain, for the Dutch Robinson Crusoe had, of course, his diary to make entries. But from the cave, looking between the hills, the sea was visible as a glittering surface in the distance and for a short time I felt like the man who looked at the horizon in the entrance of his cave, hoping to see the sails of a ship. How many times had he stood there on the lookout, in vain?

Michiel Koolbergen wanted the true story of the Dutch castaway on Ascension, after so many legends during more than 270 years, to be on the shelves of the public library of the island. Unfortunately, he died too early for that, on 1 June 2002, at the age of only 48. It was an honour and a pleasure for me to have disclosed Koolbergen's research in English with this book that will find its way to the library on Ascension.

*Ascension, seen from the southwest with Ascension Frigatebirds (*Fregata aquila*) (drawing by Anneke de Vries, from a photo by the author on board the Royal Mail Ship* Saint Helena*)*

LITERATURE

Aerts, T.M. "Het verfoeijlijcke crimen van sodomie"; Sodomie op VOC-schepen in de 18e eeuw", *Leidschrift*, April1988, pp 5-21

An Authentick Relation of the many Hardships and Sufferings of a Dutch Sailor, Who was put on Shore on the uninhabited Isle of Ascension, by Order of the Commadore of a Squadron of Dutch Ships. – with – A Remarkable Account of his Converse with Apparitions and Evil Spirits, during his Residence on the Island. - and – A particular Diary of his Transactions from the Fifth of May to the Fourteenth of October, on which Day he perished in a miserable Condition. – Taken from the Original Journal found in his Tent by some Sailors, who landed from on Board the Compton, Captain Morson Commander, in January 1725/6. London, 1728 (also Dublin, 1728)

Agnos, Peter, *The Queer Dutchman*, 1993 (first published 1978)

Ashmole, Philp and Myrtle, *St Helena and Ascension Island: a natural history*, 2000

Behrens, C.F., *Reise durch die Sued-Laender und um die Welt*, 1737

Behrens, C.F., *Histoire de l'expédition de trois vaisseaux, envoyés par la Compagnie des Indes Occidentales des Provinces-Unies, aux Australes en MDCCXXI*, 1739

Breuning, H.A., *Het voormalige Batavia*, 1954

Cross, Tony, *St Helena; including Ascension Island and Tristan da Cunha*, 1980

Dampier, William, *A voyage to New Holland, 1699-1701*, 1906

Day, Alan, *St Helena, Ascension and Tristan da Cunha*, from the World Bibiographical Series, 1997

Defoe, Daniel, *An Essay on the History and Reality of Apparitions. Being An Account of what they are, and what they are not. As Also How we may distinguish between the*

Apparitions of Good and Evil Spirits, and how we ought to behave to them. With a great Variety of Surprizing and Diverting Examples, never Publish'd before, 1727

Defoe, Daniel, *Robinson Crusoe*, 1946 (first published 1719)

Edwards, Hugh, *The Wreck on the Half-Moon Reef*, 1971

Gaastra, Femme S., *De geschiedenis van de VOC*, 1991

Hart-Davis, Duff, *Ascension, the story of a South Atlantic island*, 1972

Huxley, Roger, *Ascension Island and Turtles*, 1997 (pamphlet by the Ascension Island Heritage Society)

Iongh, D.de, *Het krijgswezen onder de V.O.C.*, 1950

Jacobs, Els M., *De Vereenigde Oost-Indische Compagnie*, 1997

The Just Vengeance of Heaven Exemplify'd. In a Journal Lately Found by Captain Mawson (Commander of the Ship Compton), on the Island of Ascension, As he was Homeward-bound from India. In which is a full and exact relation of the Author's being set on Shore there (by Order of the Commodore and Captains of the Dutch Fleet), for a most Enormous Crime he had been guilty of, and the extreme and unparallel'd Hardships, Sufferings and Misery he endur'd from the Time of his being left there, to that of his Death. All Wrote with his own Hand, and found lying near the Skeleton. London, 1730 (also Philadelphia, 1748)

Koolbergen, Michiel, *Een Hollandse Robinson Crusoë. Dagboek van de verbannen VOC-dienaar Leendert Hasenbosch op het onbewoonde eiland Ascension A.D. 1725*, 2002

Leslie, Edward E., *Desperate Journeys, Abandoned Souls; True Stories of Castaways and Other Survivors*, 1988

MacFall, Neil, *Ascension Island: A Visitor's Guide*, 2005

MacFall, Neil, *Ascension Island Walks Book*, 1998

Mare, Walter de la, *Desert Islands*, 1988 (first print 1930)

Maxwell, Constantina, *Dublin under the Georges*, 1997 (first print 1956)

Meer, Theo van der, *Sodoms zaad in Nederland*, 1995

Neider, Charles, *Great Shipwrecks and Castaways; Authentic Accounts of Adventures at Sea*, 2000 (first print 1952)

Osbeck, P., *Reise nach Ostindien und China*, 1765

Packer, J.E., *The Ascension Handbook; a concise guide to Ascension Island South Atlantic*, 1968

Roos, Doeke, *Zeeuwen en de VOC*, 1988

Saher, H.von, *Emmanuel Rodenburg, of wat er op het eiland Bali geschiedde toen de eerste Nederlanders daar in 1597 voet aan wal zetten*, 1986

Schafer, Kevin, *Ascension Island, Atlantic Outpost*, 2004

Souhami, Diana, *Selkirk's Island*, 2001

Stonehouse, Bernard, *Wideawake Island; The Story of the B.O.U. Centenary Expedition to Ascension*, 1960

Sutherland, James, *Daniel Defoe; A Critical Study*, 1971

Websites

Ascension conservation, www.conservation.org.ac
Ascension government, www.ascension-island.gov.ac
Ascension Heritage Society, www.heritage.org.ac
especially http://www.heritage.org.ac/avis1.htm;
Ascension links page www.websmith.demon.co.uk/ascensionisland

About the Marine Turtle Research Group, www.seaturtle.org/mtrg/
About the maroonings on Juan Fernandez Island around 1700,
http://academic.brooklyn.cuny.edu/english/melani/novel_18c/defoe/selkirk.html#dampier .
About gay and lesbian history,
http://www.gayhistory.com/rev2/events/1730.htm
and http://www.iisg.nl/staff/tvm.php

Website of the author:
www.aworldofislands.com

Website of the artist:
http://www.annekedevries.nl/